# Seller Financing on Steroids

Pumping Paper for
Power, Peace and Profits

(A.K.A. *"When Banks Say No, I Say Yes!"*)

## Dawn Rickabaugh

**Note Queen / Rickabaugh Realty**

# Seller Financing on Steroids:

## *Pumping Paper for Power, Peace and Profits*

ISBN: 978-1-45377-691-9

Published by:
Note Queen

www.NoteQueen.com

10  9  8  7  6  5  4  3  2
PRINTED IN THE UNITED STATES OF AMERICA

## BEFORE YOU CREATE A NOTE,
## READ THIS ONE!

This publication is intended for information purposes only. It is sold with the understanding that the publisher shall not be liable for any losses, claims, debts or demands related to this publication.

The publisher is not offering legal or accounting services. Laws, rules and regulations vary from state to state, and readers are advised to consult with their attorneys and accountants before buying or selling property or paper.

## SPECIAL THANKS

To Terese, my
Little Arrangement...
Thank you for your love,
support and inspiration
for 16 years and counting,
and to our children,
Heather, Kristi,
Lars and Lauren
(and you, too, Meesh Meesh!)

# CONTENTS

*"I loved how complete Seller Financing on Steroids was! I love IRS tax issues with Residential Property and selling property creatively (wraps-AITDs, etc). Violating the due on sale clause when selling creatively is worry for many sellers. Your solutions seem elegant, with Trusts. Minimizing or Eliminating the Capital Gains tax over the $500,000 Exclusion with an Installment Sale is also "The Complete Look" at selling a home over $500K in California. Again, best book on seller financing I have seen, especially relevant for today's market! Best to you Dawn."*

– Brian Gibbons (25 year financing vet)

\*\*\*\*\*\*\*\*\*\*\*\*

*"Seller Financing on Steroids was very informative & helpful. I wish that I read it before I agreed to terms on my first owner financed deal. I would have paid more attention to term length and interest rate. But I'm glad that I read it before the actual contract and mortgage have been drawn up. Thanks"*

– Bruce

\*\*\*\*\*\*\*\*\*\*\*\*

*"After the meeting, my clients told me they were very happy that we had gotten together. They understand how effective and important you are in this transaction and are looking forward to working with you. They were very impressed with your knowledge and the clarity of your information, especially with the various options that were discussed. Now to find the buyer and put together a plan that works for both buyer and seller."*

– Kathryn – Studio City, CA (listing agent $6M property)

\*\*\*\*\*\*\*\*\*\*\*\*

*"Thanks so much, will review with my husband when he gets in. I told him earlier today I found your website with so much information. What a blessing you are to share with so many people in such a trying time."*

– Joy

# PREFACE

At least I did something typical and conventional and mainstream, like have an all-out midlife crisis at 39-and-a-half.

I still have my nursing license, but more than 6 years ago I started out on an adventure, without compass or canteen, and this book is proof of it, or at leat a blip on the radar to prove I was here, or there, or whatever.

I was always inspired by a quote by Anais Nin that became an incessant mantra inside my head just before I quit my nice, comfortable 6-figure job:

> *"…and the day came that the pain of remaining tight*
> *in a bud was greater than the risk it took to open."*

At some point, whether by internal pressures or external forces, we all get to come to that point where we decide whose voice we're going to follow. The tectonic plates of our lives start shifting, and we get to dig through the rubble and accept or reject the invitation to explore and follow our deepest calling.

(Now, if someone would just hand out little 3x5 cards with our deepest callings typed out neatly, doubled spaced… that would be extremely helpful.)

My journey started out when I began studying the discounted note business. It fascinated and intrigued me, and I felt intelligent and accomplished when I could operate a financial calculator with even a small degree of proficiency.

I bought many courses, attended many seminars, spent too much money, and fell flat on my face for a long time.

Eventually I thought, "Well, if I'm going to work in the note business in California, it would probably be a good idea for me to get my real estate license."

So I did. And then I needed some place to hang it. So I went around interviewing mortgage and real estate offices, each time leaving with a feeling of nausea, and an insidious, creeping awareness that I probably just didn't ft in anywhere.

Then, one day I was calling real estate investors who advertised in the local paper (something I was trained to do in the note business), and I got a guy named Jerry on the phone.

Something in his voice struck a chord, so I went, scared, green, wet behind the ears, feigning a confidence I certainly didn't have.

He became a mentor and dear friend, and for three years I worked for his investment firm and cut my teeth in real estate as an agent and investor.

In the course of chasing properties to rehab and flip, I made lots of cold calls to people who owned investment properties, and I started to notice a pattern. Even if they were tired of managing and wanted to sell, many wouldn't because they:

- didn't want to pay capital gains (and didn't want to exchange)
- needed the income for retirement
- wanted to leave a good inheritance

This is where the note business and the real estate business started to merge for me. These sellers obviously didn't know about the Installment Sale (carrying back a note), because it addressed each of these concerns, plus it gave them liquidity (the ability to raise lump sums of cash by selling all or part of their note).

In those days, the height of easy financing when all you needed was a pulse to get a loan, seller financing was not needed as a tool to close real estate transactions, but was a great estate planning tool that no one seemed to know anything about.

Engineered correctly, it could safely deliver hassle-free retirement income, and liberate tired property owners who no longer had the health or inclination to deal with toilets, tenants or taxes.

When I could address their concerns, I was able to put transactions together.

Incidentally, because of my incessant whine about seller financing and creating seller carry back notes every time we discussed a real estate deal in the office, a gay associate jokingly dubbed me the "Note Queen".

****************

With the state of affairs these days, when we can't necessarily trust governments, corporations or financial institutions to protect and take care of us, there are fewer perceived illusions of safety and security to tempt us away from finding our own answers, and following our own true paths in our real estate dealings, or in anything else in our lives.

And there's a larger picture…if we're not too busy jostling for position on the deck of the Titanic, we find that it's hard to ignore certain global trends that directly affect our survival on the planet.

I'm reading a book right now that I would highly recommend, "WorldShift 2012: Making Green Business, New Politics & Higher Consciousness Work Together" by Ervin Laszlo.

Since I've already endured the discomfort of completely unravelling and rebuilding my professional and personal life over the last 6 years, what can it hurt to reinvent it a little more?

How can I incorporate ideals of sustainability, well-being and peace into every part of my life, and make it so everyone else has a shot at it, too?

It's an attitude of flexibility and creativity and being willing to scrutinize, and possibly change, beliefs and assumptions that have infiltrated us at the cellular level. And in case you're wondering, that's what this book is about... applied to the real estate arena.

What I have become committed to at this point in my life is liberating people from their own perceived limitations when it comes to real estate, money and notes.

**When banks say "NO," I say "YES."**

Helping people unplug from a system that is not serving them and empowering them to get what they want anyway... now that's fun.

When a deal is getting ready to fall out of escrow, and I get to ride in on a big white horse and put it back together, saving the seller, the buyer and the real estate agent his commission, then I'm thrilled.

I want people to understand that they are freer than than they may have thought; that they don't have to wait on anyone or anything to 'save' them.

There are many legal, ethical and intelligent options (that have nothing to do with bank financing) for selling property, buying property, creating hassle-free retirement income, getting around life-throttling capital gains, and for turning property and/or paper into the cash that will launch and support people into the next meaningful chapter of their lives.

Perhaps I should have just introduced myself as a dance instructor. I want you to learn and love "the dance between property and paper."

When you understand a little about how the secondary market determines the value of a note, then you automatically know how to structure a seller financing transaction in a way that preserves the seller's asset now and into the future.

And if you're a professional, such as a real estate agent, accountant or attorney, then knowing this information will not only elevate you in the eyes of your client, but probably keep you from getting sued (and possibly unveil profit opportunities you have long been overlooking).

Understanding TValue and how to print an amortization schedule does not mean you know how to create a note the market will pay top dollar for. I've looked at plenty of notes created by attorneys, accountants and escrow companies that contain major flaws.

Who wants a client coming back to them years down the road, screaming about how they can't sell their note, or that they're taking a huge discount because of the way a transaction was engineered? Why wouldn't you want someone to help underwrite the deal with both short and long term objectives in mind?

Thanks for staying with me so far. I've heard that 90% of the people who buy this book will never read it.

Put on your dancing shoes, and let's get busy. It's very possible that you'll get one or two ideas that will change the way you think about real estate, notes and your financial future forever.

Using a combination of owner financing, private money and commercial hedge funds in intelligent and intentional ways, we can learn to preserve assets and design a future that is sustainable, abundant and full of hope and possibility.

# INTRODUCTION

Let's face it...the real estate market just isn't functioning that well overall. Hardly a week goes by that I don't hear a disaster story about how difficult, if not impossible, bank loans are to get these days.

Even with government (taxpayer) stimuli, the credit market is still in hangover mode...throbbing headache, looking for a greasy burger and a strong cup of coffee.

Even good, qualified buyers are having a hard time qualifying for loans, especially jumbos and commercial, and many of the escrows that are lucky enough to open end up falling apart. This is doubly true for people trying to get financing to buy a small business opportunity.

Increasingly, sellers are looking for ways to get the highest possible price for their property (or business) at a time when short sales and REOs, depreciation and tight credit markets are making it hard to move anything.

Many people are rightly turning to seller financing (owner financing, seller carry back, carrying paper) to get the benefits they're looking for, but most do not understand which strategy would work best for them, and how to structure the transaction for maximum protection and profit.

This book is to help you intelligently and powerfully put a seller financing deal together that meets your needs (or the needs of your client) now and into the future.

If you're a buyer, you need to know this stuff, but you don't have to be perfect to buy with seller financing...you'll need to use the strategies I'm going to talk about and tweak them for your side of the equation. If you get stuck, call me.

# Can I offer seller financing if I already have a loan on my property?

Yes! If you've got good underlying financing, and you're willing to leave it in place for the next buyer, you can offer owner financing. But that's illegal, isn't it?

I'm surprised when people tell me this with conviction. If there is underlying bank financing, it may be a breach of contract to transfer title to the property (which gives them the right to accelerate), but it's not illegal, except in Michigan (see below). If it was illegal to 'wrap' underlying financing, then I'm quite confident that CAR's (California Association of Realtor's) legal documents would not include this option on the Seller Financing Addendum.

The bank's position is still secured by a deed of trust or mortgage, and is often more secure, as the new owner is often much more capable of maintaining the payments than the person who sold the property simply to get out from under payments that had become oppressive for them.

That said, since 1985, Michigan has had legislation penalizing licensed persons (Realtors, title companies, etc.) from participating in transfers that attempt to circumvent a DOS (Due-On-Sale) clause. Title companies will usually insure a 'Subject-To' or 'Wrap', but stipulate exclusions to coverage and require that lots of disclosures are signed by all parties.

So, there may be some legal ambiguity. If we polled 100 attorneys, some would say it's illegal (because of the one state's precedent), but many would say that it's not. You should get your own legal advice and ultimately, only do what you're comfortable with. When there is underlying bank financing, I believe the best strategy may be the Title Holding (Land) Trust.

So...what's 'good underlying financing'?

If the loan that you are paying on is a low, long-term, fixed product, then you have 'good underlying financing'. An example would be a 5.5% 30-year fixed.

That means your interest rate is **low** and **fixed** at 5.5% (it will never increase, even if interest rates go through the roof), and it's **long-term** (you have this loan for the next 30 years... you don't have to pay it off for a very long time, or refinance because of a balloon payment in 3 years).

When you are leaving existing financing in place, you will either use a:

- 'wrap' (AITD – All Inclusive Deed of Trust),
- lease option,
- contract for deed, or
- title holding (land) trust

Which strategy you use will depend on the deal and how much risk tolerance you have. We'll go over this more in the section on 'Various and Sundry Owner Financing Strategies.'

When most people hear 'seller financing,' they usually think of carrying a small 'second' after the buyer gets a regular loan. A 2nd note and deed of trust is the difference between the buyer's down payment, and the loan they are able to qualify for.

For example:

| | |
|---|---|
| Sales price: | $350,000 |
| Down payment: | $20,000 |
| Bank loan 1st: | $280,000 |
| **Seller carry back 2nd:** | **$50,000** |

This can work (unless the bank won't let another loan be recorded against the property), but if you're the seller, you just need to understand that this is strictly a gamble.

If you get your payments on the note, great! If you don't, then just know you're probably going to walk away. It won't be worth the money or hassle to keep a large 1st current while you foreclose on a small 2nd, unless we're in a rapidly appreciating market (which, um, news flash...we're not).

For this reason, a small 2nd like this will have absolutely NO VALUE in the secondary market. This means you won't be able to sell it for cash...OK, maybe $1, but that's tops.

But it can still make sense, because what's the alternative? If you don't grant this buyer a $50,000 2nd, then you'll fall out of escrow and be hanging out on the market again for who knows how long waiting for another buyer, or you'll have to do a massive price reduction. Sure, there are risks to selling and carrying a 2nd, but there are also...

*Risks of NOT selling:*
- extended DOM (days on market) – how many more mortgage payments will you make waiting for the next buyer?
- the risk of further depreciation in the market (triggering more price reductions)

- renting it out instead, possibly accepting a negative cash flow and the fact that you'll have a lot of repairs to make after your tenants are gone
- inflation – in my mind it's not a matter of 'if,' but 'when.' Sure you can hang out for the perfect buyer in the perfect market and get your price, but your dollars will be buying you less and less, so the sooner you sell for a fair price, the better. In fact, **selling for less NOW can ultimately give you more VALUE than selling for more LATER.**

So, taking back a 2nd can be an acceptable risk, because at least you have **the chance** of collecting the equity you want.

# What is seller financing and how does it work?

Ok, down to the basics.

I guess on the surface, it could sound like seller financing is where the seller of a property goes out and gets a bank loan and gives it to the buyer so they have the cash to buy the property, but NO, that's NOT what seller financing means (although there are strategies we'll talk about later that almost seem like that).

When you own a property, you either have a loan against it, or you don't. If you don't, then you own your property 'free and clear.' (And by the way, congratulations! You may be interested in the chapter about deferring capital gains).

If your property is worth $200,000 and you own it free and clear, then you have 100% equity, or $200,000 in equity that you could potentially 'loan' to a prospective buyer.

If you have a 50% LTV (loan-to-value) loan against your property (i.e. a $100,000 loan on your $200,000 property), then you have 50% equity, or $100,000 in equity to loan.

*Your EQUITY (and/or your existing financing) is what you can potentially 'loan' to a prospective buyer.*

That is how you, as the seller/owner, are providing the financing.

So, instead of having the buyer go out and get a bank loan, **you become the bank**. You will take a down payment from the buyer AND receive the monthly payments from the buyer as they pay you for your property in installments (little bits at a time).

That's why seller financing is also known as an installment sale...the buyer is paying for your property in monthly installments (plus interest). This is why the IRS (according to IRC 453) allows you to defer capital gains when you carry paper.

Because you are collecting the payment for your property a little at a time, Uncle Sam says, "OK, since you are playing nice and only getting a little of your equity back at a time, we'll play nice, too, and only take our capital gains a little at a time."

That way, most of your equity can stay working for you. If you take an all cash offer, then you may have a hefty capital gains bill to pay. What if it's $200,000? Ouch! That $200,000, if left at work for you in the property, even at 6% could make you an additional **$12,000 a year** in interest!

Hey, don't knock it! That'll buy you a cappuccino and a nice bottle of wine every day for an entire year!

Let's put this another way...

Take out your deed of trust (if you have a loan against your property) and look at it. It identifies a Trustor, a Trustee, and a Beneficiary.

- If you own the property, then you are the **Trustor**. The Beneficiary is trusting you to pay back the money they lent you, but just in case you don't, they will have the Trustee repossess the security = collateral = your property to satisfy the debt.
- A title company is usually listed as the **Trustee**. This entity is responsible for foreclosing on the property

on behalf of the beneficiary if you, the Trustor, quit paying according to the terms of your promissory note. They are the Trustee for the Deed of Trust which contains a Power of Sale clause that allows them to sell your property at a Trustee's Sale.

- The **Beneficiary** is the lender, the entity that made a loan against the property, the originator of the promissory note secured by a deed of trust against your property.

When you offer seller financing, then you put on a different hat. Instead of being the Trustor, you play the role of the Beneficiary. You didn't lend the Trustor (the buyer that now owns your property) money, but you lent them your **equity**.

And if they don't pay you your remaining equity according to the note(s) as promised (promissory note), then the Trustee will foreclose and give the property back to you (if you pay them a nice chuck of change to do it, of course).

*Story time:*

A cute little old couple owned a commercial building down the street from my house. They had run a travel agency business out of it for over 25 years, but one day as we passed it to get our afternoon coffee, we noticed a handwritten sign on the back door that said: FOR SALE BY OWNER.

My partner needed an art studio, but we knew we would never qualify for a commercial loan, and that we needed the property to carry itself (with a mortgage at home and 4 kids to feed, we didn't need another expense).

But what could we lose? I picked up the phone and called John.

It was like negotiating with my grandparents. They were so kind and polite, and Patricia always wore a purple knit hat and kept trying to give me old magazines she'd collected. (One day I'm going to proudly sport a little purple hat and play lead guitar in a rock band).

The best part about it was that they insisted on carrying paper. I couldn't have enticed them with all cash or a juicy bank loan if I'd wanted to. They wanted to play the role of the juicy banker.

***Seller financing was a major part of their retirement plan.***

They owned the property free and clear, and they wanted 20% down and would carry at 7.5%, amortized over 30 years, due in 15.

They placed a 25% pre-payment penalty on it for the first 10 years so I couldn't pay the loan off early, because if they got paid off early, they would have a big capital gains liability, and it would defeat their reason for carrying paper in the first place. At the time, bank CD's were paying all of 2-3%, so the strategy made a lot of sense.

Ultimately, they took 15% down, and carried at 3.75% for the first 18 months, and 7.5% thereafter.

Here's what it looked like:

| | |
|---|---|
| Sales price: | $370,000 |
| Down payment: | $50,000 |
| First note and deed of trust: | $320,000 |
| Interest rate: | 3.75%, then 7.5% |

Term: amortized over 360, due in 180
Monthly payment: $1,481.97 (first 18 months)
$2,206.28 (thereafter)

So, they got $50,000 down and now they get $2,206.28 every month from me, which is basically their pension fund/

retirement plan. I guess that's lucky for them, because if they'd have had their nest egg in the stock market like many people did, they'd have lost half of it by now, and be wondering where their next TV dinner was going to come from.

If they'd have sold for all cash, they'd have paid about $70,000 in capital gains, and had $300,000 to stick in a bank CD at 2.5%.

Let's see:

| | |
|---|---|
| Principal: | $300,000 |
| Interest rate: | 2.5% |
| Monthly interest: | $625 |

Instead they only paid about $12,000 in capital gains, had enough money left over from the down payment to pay off the remaining mortgage on their home, and they get $2,206.28 per month instead of $625. Not bad.

And it's worked perfectly for us, because we collect $2,950 a month plus utilities from the downstairs tenants in the building, so all we're left with covering is the insurance, about $350 a month. That's much less than we would have paid just trying to rent an 1,100 sqft art studio somewhere.

Now, I've got the property up for sale, because it won't be long before all the kids are out of high school, and we're planning our escape.

I'm offering it as a sale-lease-back, because we still need to use the upstairs unit for another couple of years, but I'd like to increase my cash flow from the property and reduce my exposure to potential vacancy if my tenants ever decide to call it quits.

But remember that pre-payment penalty? And guess what? I have no intention of paying capital gains right now. So here's the current description on my listing:

*"Owner will carry. No bank financing needed. Beautiful 2-story commercial building in the heart of Temple City. Owner is looking for a sale-leaseback, intending to retain leasehold of the 2nd level for approximately 3 years. Seller must carry, terms flexible. Open to lease option, contract for deed, or partnership in a title holding (land) trust to preserve existing tax basis and defer capital gains."*

Here's how the deal could end up looking if we use the Title Holding (Land) Trust:

| | |
|---|---|
| Purchase price or MAV: | $947,000 |
| (mutually agreed value) | |
| Down payment or Initial Contribution: | $150,000 |
| Remaining amount: | $797,000 |
| Interest rate: | 7% |
| Term: amortized over 240, due in 60 | |
| **Monthly payment (lease payment):** | **$6,179.13** |

So, instead of the building just barely carrying itself, we could pocket $3,972.85 each month instead ($6,179.13 minus the $2,206.28 I owe to my 'grandparents'). The 'buyer' would cover taxes and insurance, maintenance and repairs, and worry about any potential vacancies.

And out of that $150,000 down payment, I won't pay a lick of capital gains. I won't pay any taxes until the trust is terminated 5 years from now, and even then, **I may decide to 1031 exchange my beneficial interest in the land trust for another 'like kind' investment for 100% deferral of capital gains and depreciation recapture. That sounds kinda nice.**

The deal could be put together a hundred different ways, so it'll be fun to see how it comes together. (And I'll talk more about the Land Trust in a later section).

*Post script:*

So that was my fantasy, but I'll tell you how things ended up working out…

The commercial market softened rapidly while I was marketing the property, and instead of selling for $947,000, we closed at $680,000 – a bit of a difference, eh?

Here are some of the reasons we accepted the $680,000:
- 40% cash down payment (great owner carry potential)
- no inspection
- no contingencies
- taking the property "as is"
- 30 day escrow
- allowed us to retain a leasehold of our upstairs unit for 6 years at below-market rent (with ability to leave at any time without financial obligation)
- did not require us to evict or negotiate with any of the existing tenants
- we needed the money!

We launched into escrow before I had been able to negotiate the prepayment penalty with the estate (both sellers had died) and I had 2 years left on the prepay. The buyer was able to qualify for a very attractive SBA loan that she wanted.

(As a side note, I had decided that I would just go ahead and take the capital gains hit now, since taxes will only be going up from here).

I was naively confident that the estate would be happy to be paid off and disburse assets, and would waive the prepayment penalty. Um…it cost me $40,000 to get out of that deal. I should have had the prepay expire when the last of the note holders died…my bad.

# Am I offering seller financing for the right reasons, or because I have a bruised ego?

Because owner financing can be such a powerful tool for getting top dollar in any market, sometimes sellers go that route, even when they shouldn't. They are so attached to getting a certain dollar amount for their property, they can lose sight of the big picture. That's why I could have entitled this section:

### *So You're Stuck on Price – Let's Have a Heart to Heart (AKA: Life Coach Moment)*

Obviously, I love seller financing and real estate notes, and any non-traditional way of closing real estate transactions. I've almost made it a point of personal religion to avoid bank financing.

Owner financing is a great way to maximize price point, but is price always the most important thing? Is offering seller financing just to get the highest possible price always the right thing for people to do?

**No.**

Some people need to get top dollar because they have very little equity. They owe almost as much as their property is worth (or maybe even a little bit more), and they're trying to avoid a short sale and/or default. They at least want to take a stab at preserving their credit.

Some people own their properties free and clear, and are carrying paper as part of their retirement strategy. While they obviously want the most money possible, safety, monthly cash flow and deferring capital gains is the most important conversation.

Some people need top dollar because, literally, the property represents their life savings, and they need to salvage every penny they can out of it. (And if that's you, make sure you REALLY structure the transaction carefully so you can sleep at night and eat more than cat food the next morning.)

And some people want to offer seller financing just to get a price that's stuck in their heads, because they don't want to 'lose money.' Their egos just won't allow them to 'take a loss.' They don't want to look silly, feel foolish or play the part of a chump.

It's these people that I want to chat with for a moment. Or maybe I'll just tell you a quick story...

### Story time:

Harvey and Hedwig heard about what I'd done for Heinrich (you'll read about him later), and contacted me for help with their million dollar property.

Six years previously, they had purchased a beautiful 5 acre estate, and had been pouring love and cash into it ever since. A year before they flew me up for a consultation, Realtors had pegged the value of their home somewhere between $1.2 and $1.5 million. Now, the numbers were coming in below a million, and it was just more than they could stand.

So, they decided that they would hire me to set up a seller financing transaction so they could maximize the price they could get for the property.

Great! I'm all over that! Because they had attractive underlying financing in place, I knew I could safely put a deal together for them using the Title Holding Trust, or a 'Wrap' if the risk of acceleration was tolerable.

*While I was up there, my objectives were to:*
- Talk strategy (there's a lot to explain to people about the title holding trusts and seller financing in general)
- Interview Realtors to help them choose the right one (we needed a professional comfortable with non-traditional financing)
- See the property and take photos for an internet flyer and blog
- I even took my video camera to create a home spun virtual tour to capture the magic of the place, share the feeling of being there, and tell the story of the people and property behind the transaction

But during the course of my 2-day stay, I got to know more about them than I'd become aware of even after several phone conversations. I learned a lot more about why they were selling, and what they hoped they'd be able to do once the property was sold.

And that's when I knew we needed to have a 'Come to Jesus' talk...

Here's what I discovered that made me talk them out of using my services as a seller financing consultant: they both wanted to be out of the 'rat race,' and both were contemplating major life transitions.

Harvey wanted to go live in Spain. He wanted the freedom to live in a tiny apartment without air conditioning, and just immerse himself in the language, the culture, the people, the food...the simple goodness of living and being. Hedwig wanted to start teaching yoga while rehabilitating their Palm Springs home.

Neither of them wanted to be tied to having to make a certain amount of money each month. Although Harvey had always made good money in his business, it just didn't inspire him any more...he was ready for a whole new chapter in his life. And what would most make them feel like they could safely make these life transitions?

*Money...a big chunk of money in the bank.*

"So why then," I asked them, "Would you accept a relatively small down payment ($100,000) and carry paper on your house just to push the purchase price closer to a million than $900,000?"

After closing costs, that would only give them about $40K in the bank...not exactly the kind of money that would set their minds at ease. It would be almost impossible for them to throw themselves at their new adventures with complete abandon.

Yes, they'd have monthly cash flow, but what if something went wrong? What if the buyers got laid off from Microsoft or Zillow and couldn't make the payments? Then pretty soon that positive cash flow turns into negative cash flow, because the underlying bank loan, taxes and insurance would still have to be paid.

And what if the defaulting buyers hadn't taken good care of the place? What if they had let the landscaping dry up? Then there would be money to spend and repairs to make just to put it on the market again, and will the market be better at that time, or possibly worse?

And what if something catastrophic happened? What if a hot air balloon crashed into the house? It would be hard to recover that thinly won equity.

The potential for loss is too great with only a 10% down payment, and it just wouldn't be worth it, especially when their whole way of life could be compromised. It would be a different story if the equity tied up in the property didn't represent such a significant amount of their net worth.

If they just listed and sold at $900,000 to a 'regular' buyer, then they would have closer to $250,000 in the bank...now that starts to sound a little better. It sounded to me like selling for $900,000 to a conventional buyer who could qualify for traditional financing would meet their true objectives better than getting $1,000,000 a little at a time.

But that ego thing is a tough one. It can spew out all sorts of arguments that tempt you to trade in your dreams for shallow satisfactions and the promise of just a little more money. It rambles on:

> *"But it was worth $1.2mil just last year, and I don't think the market has fallen that far, and I don't want to just give the property away."*

The ego likes to believe that there must be some conspiracy going on, that the real estate professionals providing comparable market data must be sitting in dark alleys, calculating ways to rob it of its just rewards.

I went on to torture him with an especially annoying line of questioning...

> **"And what would it mean if you were to 'give the property away' at $900,000?"**

*"Well that would mean that someone is taking advantage of me."*

**"And what does it mean if someone takes advantage of you?"**

*"Well, that means I wasn't very smart…that I was naive and incompetent. You know, the last property I sold increased $200K in value after I sold it…I'm not going to be that stupid again. I vowed I would make up for that 'loss' with this property."*

**"Now, you sold your business at the top of the market a couple of years ago, right? I mean, you couldn't have timed that sale any better, could you?"**

*"No, I hit that one just perfect. I could see the trends that were coming, and I sold just before the economy started tanking."*

**"So in one instance you hit the top of the market and sold for top dollar, and in the other, you didn't. So one transaction made you feel like a genius, the other a total failure."**

And that's what most of us do…we let the profits we make or lose directly determine our sense of self worth. We act like suffering a financial loss is a shameful, dark family secret…dirty laundry that must be buried in some corner of the collective subconscious until some future generation airs it out and sets it free.

Harvey just had too much baggage attached to his property, and it was compromising his ability to make a sane decision. He was spending a lot of time and energy (and he was willing to risk everything) just to avoid 'taking a loss,' because somehow that would be conclusive evidence that he is indeed a dunce. But check this out…did he really ever even take a loss?

His last property he bought for $500,000 and sold for $650,000. A couple of years later, the subsequent owner sold it for $850,000. So naturally, Harvey logged that in as a $200,000 loss when in reality, he made a $150,000 profit.

He bought their current property for $600,000, they put $200,000 into it, and now the market says it's worth $900,000. But instead of feeling like he's sitting on a $100,000 profit, he insists that he's taking a $300,000 loss because he could have sold it last year for $1,200,000.

*Whew! Why do we do these kinds of things to ourselves?*

All I'm saying is, be willing to ask yourself some tough questions, and take a good hard look at what it is you really want to experience next in your life, and try not to get attached to the numbers. If you're not sure you're making the right decision, hire me to make you uncomfortable and ask you questions that will help ensure you're in alignment with your highest good.

*Protect your quality of life at least as fiercely*
*as you protect your 'profits.'*

# Various and Sundry Owner Financing Strategies

There are several owner financing strategies to choose from…they rest in front of you like dabs of paint on an artist's palette. The brush you pick up and the color you choose to stroke across your canvas will determine whether you'll end up with a masterpiece that will hang proudly and fit perfectly in your living room, or a bad craft project you'll end up wanting to shove your foot through.

Putting together an owner financing transaction is an art form. There are an unbelievable amount of factors that must be accounted for if all parties are to be properly educated, satisfied and protected, now and into the future.

And it's impossible to list all the variables. Every transaction is unique. That's why **consulting** with someone who understands real estate, as well as real estate notes, along with a pinch of financial planning will REALLY make a HUGE difference in how your deal turns out.

**[And it helps to choose someone who can act as a life coach (who may perhaps make you a little uncomfortable) and help you get at the root of what it is you really need, not what you think you want.]**

OK, so let's talk briefly about the major strategies out there:

    1. Installment Sale – (Seller Financing)
    2. The 'wrap' or AITD (All Inclusive Deed of Trust)

3. 'Subject To'
4. Title Holding (Land) Trust
5. Lease Option or Lease Purchase
6. Contract for Deed (Sales Contract/Land Contract)

## 1. Installment Sale – (Seller Financing)

I think we've covered this quite nicely already...no need to waste any more space. I'm mainly thinking of those properties that have no existing financing (the owner owns them free and clear), or the situations where the buyer gets a bank loan for as much as they possibly can, and then the seller carries back a 2nd.

Pretty straight forward. The deed is transferred to the buyer upon close of escrow, just like in a 'regular' sale. The next two are just variations of the installment sale. (and yes, buyers can qualify for the tax credit on owner-financed properties)

## 2. The 'wrap' or AITD (All Inclusive Deed of Trust)

This is where the seller has existing financing on the property that he intends to leave in place. He'll take the down payment and create a note that is larger than, and which incorporates, the existing note. The new financing wraps around the old financing like the flesh of an olive around its pit.

This is easy to do with private notes, especially if there's no DOS (Due-On-Sale) clause. Remember the example in the beginning? I was talking about the commercial building I have for sale that has an existing seller financed note on it. If I wanted to wrap the underlying financing, I could, and here's how it could look:

**First note: $797,000 (wrapping a $320,000 note)**
**Monthly payment: $6,179.13 (wrapping a $2,206.28**
**payment)**

My monthly cash flow would be $3,972.85. If you have existing financing that contains an alienation (due on sale) clause, as most conventional financing does these days, you may get away with a wrap, you may not.

The bank will eventually find out that a title transfer has occurred, and when they do, they may do nothing, or they may decide that their reserves are uncomfortably low and decide to 'call in' everything they can. Then, things will get complicated if the financing can't be easily replaced.

A wrap is easy and cheap, but I wouldn't do it if any of the parties to the transaction would be financially injured upon acceleration. If you've got cash or a rich and generous relative, then don't worry about it. If the loan gets called, you can just pay it off.

If you can't afford for anything to happen to the underlying financing, then you'll want to consider using a Title Holding (Land) Trust. It's not a panacea, but gives you the strongest defensible position from which to negotiate.

P.S. A wrap/AITD is a great way to solve a Mortgage Over Basis problem when it comes to capital gains on an investment property. You just have to get the underlying lender to provide you with a written waiver promising not to accelerate the loan.

And remember…any time there's a 'wrap,' you must have a servicing or escrow company to keep everybody honest!

[Review pages 1 & 2 to remind yourself of issues related to 'Wraps' and Due-On-Sale clauses].

### 3. 'Subject To'

Please don't try this at home. A 'subject to' purchase option actually used to be included in the official CAR (California Association of Realtors) documents years ago, but it confused everyone, so they eventually removed it.

And I don't think there's ever a reason to use it. It leaves the seller wide open if the buyer quits making the payments. How do I know to avoid this like the plague?

Because I used this once, and although everything turned out alright in the end, it was too stressful along the way, and at 46, I just don't need another reason for grey hair and wrinkles. I'm in that, "Do everything to hang onto my youth," mode, and reducing stress is part of my plan.

'Subject to' is when the buyer buys a property 'subject to' the existing financing. They take over making payments on the loan that is already in place, and if there's extra equity, then the buyer also makes a monthly payment to the seller on a 2nd note and deed of trust. If the buyer is on the up and up, then everything works out.

But if the buyer/payor stops making the payments, how long will it take you to find out, and what are you going to do? You can't foreclose to regain possession unless he stops paying on a 2nd he owes you.

**Your name is on the loan, but you can't get control of the property**, which won't make you very happy, unless you have nothing to lose and you were ready to ditch the property anyway.

Even if you intend to give the buyer the advantage of the balance and terms of your existing loan, still do a wrap (or better yet, use the land trust idea). You'll have more control.

You can just make your wrap identical to the terms of your original loan.

***************

OK...so that 'wraps' up the conversation to this point. In each of the above examples, title is transferred to the buyer at close of escrow. In the following strategies, title is not transferred to the buyer until a later date.

## 4. Title Holding (Land) Trust

The "Illinois" Title Holding (Land) Trust is a revocable, inter-vivos, beneficiary-directed trust that is accepted in most parts of the country (works very well in 39 out of the 50 states), and is a great asset preservation tool.

There are all sorts of professionals from MLS CEOs to attorneys that contend that the trust concept is illegal and fraudulent (when intended to ultimately transfer ownership), yet there are many attorneys and brokers who support and put these transactions together on a regular basis. I know of a Keller Williams office that is routinely working with land trusts for their investor clients on a massive scale.

You can be fraudulent with anything and everything, but if your intent is asset preservation and all parties are dealt with ethically and honestly, then there is no evidence the title holding trust is going anywhere soon. Too many politicians benefit from it! (Did I say that out loud?)

*The benefits of the Title Holding Trust usually include:*
- Asset preservation & privacy of ownership
- Powerful and simple estate planning
- Defer capital gains (and depreciation recapture) until the trust is terminated (anywhere from 1 to 20 years)

- Under most circumstances, a beneficial interest in a land trust may be exchanged for other 'like-kind' real property without recognition of gain or loss under the IRC's Section 1031
- Best defense against a lender exercising a "due on sale" clause on residential (1-4) properties
- Eliminates exposure to foreclosure
- Be able to evict a defaulting "resident beneficiary" according to tenant law
- Reduces the risk of taking a small down payment, (or providing a private loan where the LTV is higher than you're comfortable with)
- Protection from litigation, creditor judgments, tax liens and probate issues
- Preserve tax basis (property is not reassessed in some states)
- Acquire an interest in real property with a small initial contribution
- In some cases, freezes the seller's equity until some point in the future when housing has begun to appreciate again (the seller has a chance of collecting 'perceived' equity at some point in the future instead of writing it off completely right now because of market conditions)
- Retain an equitable interest in the property when the buyer's bank won't allow you to record a 2nd seller carry against your property

When writing about land trust practice for the Illinois Institute for Continuing Legal Education in 1974, attorney Henry W. Kenoe wrote:

*"No arrangement of legal interests could have attained the popularity and wide usage accorded the*

*land trusts unless its applications were practical and responsive to the needs of those dealing in real estate interests."*

Extensive discussion of land trust applications are found in: Department of Conservation v. Franzen, 43 Ill. App. 3d 374, 356 N.E.&d 1245, 1 Ill. Dec 912 (1976). These discussions indicate that the land trust (Title Holding Trust) offers multiple advantages "...not available otherwise..." in a less complex and simplified form.

As recently as 1994, attorney F. Bentley Mooney, Jr. wrote an article in the well-respected Commercial Investment Real Estate Magazine: **"Protect Your Assets With a Land Trust."**

There are ways to put a trust together cheaply, especially if you're simply taking title in the name of a trust and you're going to remain the sole beneficiary.

But, if you have a multi-party trust where unrelated beneficiaries are coming together, then it's worth the price to have someone help you engineer it. There are numerous points of negotiation that most people are not aware of (until it's too late), and you absolutely must work with a company that pays attention to evolving case law. You've got to know you have the maximum protections incorporated into your trust documents.

Unfortunately, there are some proponents of the trust out there that are a bit cavalier in their approach, somewhat careless in implementation, and making promises and guarantees that they probably should not be making.

If there is existing financing being left in place for the benefit of the beneficiaries, then you'll want a trustee who also handles bill paying, so all parties know that the financial obligations are being taken care of.

Many private investors are willing to make attractive 'soft money' loans, especially if they're using **self-directed IRA's,** when the subject property is being held in the title holding trust. (P.S. You can also buy discounted notes through your self-directed IRA.)

*About the due-on-sale clause:*

FDIRA 1982, better known as the Garn-St. Germain Act under Title 12 USC Sec. 1701-j-3, allows lenders to enter into and enforce loan contracts containing a Due-On-Sale clause. There are a few exceptions to this that the Title Holding (Land) Trust takes advantage of:

- Granting of lease-hold for less than 3 years that does not involve an option to purchase, and
- Transfer into an inter vivos trust in which the borrower is and remains a beneficiary.

To be fair, there is debate as to whether Garn-St. Germain is the prevailing legal force, because it expressly allows another governing body to interpret and administer it. Garn-St-Germain (e)(1):

*The Federal Home Loan Bank Board, in consultation with the Comptroller of the Currency and the National Credit Union Administration Board, is authorized to issue rules and regulations and to publish interpretations governing the implementation of this section.*

According to conversations with friend and mentor, David Butler...

That governing body has made their interpretations in The Code of Federal Regulations, which operates as "force of law" under the Administrative Procedures Act of 1946; therefore, 12 C.F.R. PART 591, Sec. 591.5 (1) (vi), appears to be the statutory law on the matter, as things presently stand.

12 C.F.R. PART 591 basically purports that Title Holding (Land) Trusts will not be effective at getting around the Due-on-Sale clause, but it is also quite ambiguous and contradictory:

> *"The legal argument available to us is that the C.F.R. version of the inter vivos trust preemption to the DOS clause is unreasonable and clearly ambiguous, whereas Garn-St. Germain is unambiguous. That fact that the C.F.R. version is self-contradictory and nonsensical in application would seem to present a strong defense in proper use of the Title Holding Trusts. Such a defense is not available to LLC's, lease-options, land contracts, wraps, or subject-to's, so when we use the Title Holding (Land) Trust, we are still ahead of the game when done properly."* — David Butler

Part of 'done properly' means using the trust primarily for asset preservation and estate planning…as an investment strategy, and not for the sole purpose of hiding from or getting around the banks.

*What does all this mumbo jumbo mean?*

The Title Holding (Land) Trust is one of the most powerful tools out there, but **you absolutely want the right people putting your trust together for you** to assure its validity so it'll keep protecting you year after year.

*The Process:*

1. **The property seller (Settlor) vests both legal and equitable title of the property with the Trustee** of a land trust to be created, and subsequently

2. **Transfers a beneficial interest in the trust to a Resident Beneficiary** (the 'Buyer') upon mutually agreed terms and conditions of the principal parties (which usually involves a financial contribution or 'down payment')
   - Right of possession, management of the property, as well as the right to rents, issues, profits and proceeds of sale or mortgage financing are vested in the Beneficiaries.
   - The rights, privileges, duties of the Beneficiaries are NOT considered interests in real estate, but characterized as personal property (chattel).
   - The Trustee has no duties or powers other than to execute deeds and mortgages or otherwise to deal with property as directed by the Beneficiaries, who have Power of Direction
   - Power of Direction (a property interest separable from the beneficial interest), provides the possessor with ability to direct the Trustee in how to deal with the property
3. **A Beneficiary Agreement is drafted between the parties**
4. **The Resident Beneficiary (Buyer) leases the property from the Trustee** through an Occupancy or Lease Agreement.

# Anatomy of the Transaction

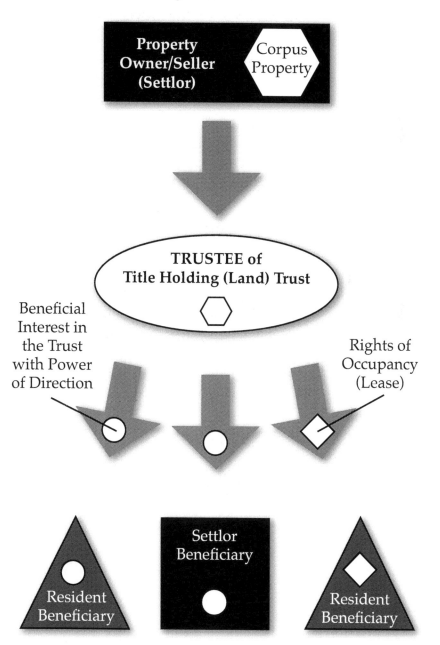

*Quick Story:*

Remember I promised to tell you about Heinrich? You know, Harvey and Hedwig's friend? Well, Heinrich owned a very expensive second home in Palm Springs. He paid $2.5mil and put another $500K into it. And then the market happened. And instead of it being easy to make that $16,000 a month mortgage payment, it was strangling him.

So, he put the house on the market for $2.9mil with a very good agent. Several months and several price reductions later, it was still sitting unsold, the listing was about to expire, and Heinrich was heading for foreclosure.

At that point, when he had nothing to lose, he was finally ready to let me advertise an alternative strategy. I explained that we would use the Title Holding Trust to help preserve his excellent financing ($1.7mil @ 6.75% fixed) to make the transaction feasible. I worked with his agent so we could coordinate, and she was cooperative and familiar with the Title Holding Trust.

We ended up finding a Canadian buyer who was very satisfied to pick up an interest in this property without new bank financing (which would be almost impossible for him to get), and Heinrich turned a pending foreclosure into a positive cash flow of almost $3,000 per month. And the agent squeaked out a commission that she was getting ready to lose, so she was thrilled!

*Another One – Take II:*

I want to share another quick story that illustrates how the Title Holding (Land) Trust helps owners of high-end luxury homes preserve their equity (get the highest possible price) at a time when prices are dropping, properties aren't appraising, and even great buyers can't get loans.

Everyone knows that you can't defer capital gains on your primary residence...all you get is the $250,000 or $500,000 homeowners 121 exclusion, right?

**Wrong.**

The Title Holding (Land) Trust is a powerful, unique way for sellers of high-end primary residences to defer capital gains. Structured properly, the seller will have the option of exchanging their beneficial interest in the trust for 'like-kind' property (which includes any typical real estate investment).

**Here's the scoop:**

Seller on the market for over 2 years without any offers. Listing price started at $2.5 mil, now it's down to $1.6 mil, and still no offers, except for someone who is willing to agree to a $1.4 mil value, but can't get bank financing.

Seller bought the property for $650,000.

Existing loan: interest-only $1 mil fixed for 4 years at 5.65%, then adjustable after that.

If seller wanted to sell at market value today to someone who could get a loan, he'd have to reduce his listing price to $1 mil, because the property wouldn't appraise for more than that right now.

In the last 18 months, only 2 listings closed over the $1 mil price point in his area. This would mean he either has to bring in money to close, or do a short sale.

**So, in order to...**

1. Preserve his $400,000 of 'equity' (equity that doesn't really exist at this point in the market), and to

2. Defer capital gains on a primary residence ($1.4 mil less $650,000 = $750,000 in taxable

gain, less $500,000 homeowner's exclusion = $250,000 in taxable gain, which would mean approximately $62,500 in tax liability), and

3. To get out from under payments that have become oppressive for him in the safest possible way, without exposure to foreclosure. (He was paying $7,000 per month and he had already bought another $2.3 mil property to live in... he was carrying 2 jumbo mortgage payments! Ouch!)

4. To make the deal even more attractive and doable, the investor/buyer gets the benefit of the existing property tax basis, which is much lower than if she were closing on the property conventionally.

**In order to achieve these benefits, the seller was happy to put the property into a Title Holding (Land) Trust:**

- MAV (mutually agreed value): $1,400,000
- Investor/buyer initial contribution: $150,000
- Buyer leases property for $7,500 /month, which covers $7,000 ITI (interest, taxes, insurance) and agrees to have the extra $500/month go towards principal reduction for the protection of all beneficiaries
- Trust term: 10 years (can be terminated earlier by mutual written consent) By then, it is hoped that either the property will have appreciated so that the investor/buyer can refinance the property and get title in their own name, or sell it to another party for a price greater than $1.4 mil.

At that point, the seller (settlor beneficiary) can exchange his beneficial interest in the trust for another like-kind property to continue to defer all of his capital gains.

## 5. Lease Option or Lease Purchase

A lease option is simply where the tenant buyer gives the owner option money up front for the right, but not the obligation, to buy the property at a specified price some time in the future.

The tenant buyer generally pays more each month than a regular tenant would, and usually a portion of each monthly lease payment is credited towards an eventual down payment if they decide to purchase.

The lease option violates a lender's due-on-sale clause, so if they found out, a bank could 'call' any underlying financing. A lease option (if an option fee is taken or rent credits given) can lead to an inability to evict a defaulting tenant.

Such a tenant in default can claim having "Equity" in the property, and in so doing, force a judicial foreclosure process versus an eviction. This can afford him/her months of free rent while the litigation rages on. As well, terms can be changed on a whim relative to buy-out provisions, repairs, equity credits (rent credits), etc.: all requiring extensive, expensive, legal action to rectify.

## 6. Contract for Deed (Sales Contract/Land Contract)

This is essentially a "Lay Away Plan." The property's legal title is relinquished to the vendee (buyer) only after all debt has been paid off: i.e., there is no legal ownership of the property until it's completely paid for.

The CFD is a direct violation of a lender's due-on-sale clause; there is no means for eviction; the vendee (resident/buyer) holds an "equitable" interest in the property, allowing only for foreclosure, ejectment and quiet title in the event of a breach of contract. Further, any parties' creditor liens, lawsuits, judgments, marital dispute litigation and tax liens attach to the property, and the death of any party throws the property into probate.

And because title is still in the name of the seller/vendor, they could potentially encumber (place more loans on the property) without the knowledge of the buyer/vendee. Additionally, the CFD no longer helps the seller defer capital gains.

****************

Of all these, I recommend the regular ol' Installment Sale (in some instances a typical wrap) but the Title Holding (Land) Trust remains one of my favorites for a lot of reasons.

# Make the Most Out of Advertising "Owner Will Carry"

There are lots of good buyers out there that just can't get a loan for one reason or another, so when you advertise "Owner Will Carry," you greatly expand the pool of potential buyers for your property.

Loans are harder to get, especially on jumbo residential and commercial (and small business), so when you take the financing dilemma out of the equation, your chances of quickly closing a satisfactory transaction greatly increase. If a buyer doesn't have to worry about jumping through a hundred hoops trying to qualify for bank financing, then they're going to be very excited to talk to you.

*Well, if they can't qualify for a bank loan,*
*are they really good buyers?*

Maybe, maybe not. But what about all those people who have ruined credit because of a divorce, or a credit card dispute, or a foreclosure because they got stuck at the top of the market with one too many investments? Are these bad buyers? Not necessarily. A low FICO doesn't always mean you should avoid business with these people. You just have to be smart about it.

Sellers are turning to non-traditional methods of closing real estate transactions because they just need to to get their deal closed, or they are doing everything they can to get the highest possible price for their property, and it's a good strategy.

But I contend you should advertise "Owner Will Carry" even if you don't intend to carry the financing for a buyer, because you will attract a lot more attention = more potential buyers = a quicker sale at a potentially higher price.

### Another Story:

I helped a successful contractor buy a good rehab fixer in a great neighborhood, but before he could start his project, his finances got stuck. Worker's Comp came in and froze all of his assets for several months.

By the time he'd completed the upgrades and repairs and actually got on the market, it had turned, and he'd lost approximately $100,000 in potential profits. So, of course, now he's just trying to break even and price point is all he's thinking about.

I knew he had excellent long-term financing that he could potentially leave in place for the next buyer, so I advised him that because he was so attached to price, he should probably offer terms.

He'd done a great job rehabbing the property, it was clean and showed extremely well, but he needed to pull out all the stops. There are tons of books out there on how to stage, prepare and market your home, but rarely do sellers realize that advertising "Owner Will Carry," "No Bank Financing Needed," is often the most powerful way to make a property more attractive and provide an edge over the competition.

He eventually succumbed to my cajoling. Even though his first choice was to get a buyer with conventional financing, he agreed to let me advertise 'Owner Will Carry' when I listed his property, not because he wanted to, but because he could.

*I've found that this type of advertising will usually double the amount of interest that I get on a property.*

We made OWC a focal point of the advertising with yard signage, in the MLS description, and on Craigslist and other internet sites.

I also talked him into listing below $500,000. He was dead set on getting $550,000, but the comps showed me it was probably only worth about $515,000. I told him if he listed at what he wanted to get, then he would languish on the market with all the other unrealistic sellers and end up losing even more money as he chased the market down.

Once again, he listened to me, but only after I hit him over the head with his own cave man club several times.

Additionally, I urged him to treat the sale of his property like an auction to create bidding fervor. For several days he basically lived at the property showing loads of prospective buyers and their agents his handiwork. We told inquiring minds that we wouldn't be reviewing offers until Friday of the following week, and advised everyone to simply submit their best offer.

Within a week, we were sitting on 25 written offers. We countered them all and were in escrow at a purchase price of $549,000 after only 10 days on the market.

And he didn't end up carrying. He accepted a conventional cash-to-new-loan offer which allowed him to liquidate his position and walk away, clean and simple, with all of his money.

There was no way that would have happened if he had listed for $549,000…probably not if he had listed for $525,000. And advertising OWC definitely got us some extra phone calls and foot traffic.

*How can you have the best chances of selling quickly for the highest possible price?*

- Offer seller financing (even if you really want a cash buyer) and make it a major focal point of your advertising:
  - Sign riders in the yard: "Owner Will Carry," or "No Bank Financing Needed," or "Special Financing Available"
  - Make sure your agent features the special terms in the description area of the listing that will get picked up by Realtor. com (you need to choose an agent who understands owner financing intimately)
  - Create nice internet flyers that get uploaded to all the home sites, including Craigslist
  - Create a mini blog for your property with lots of pictures, information, and its history, and maybe even…
  - Shoot some video. There are expensive virtual tours you can pay for, but lots of times, something personal and authentic is more effective. People emotionally relate to stories, so tell the unique story of the property, and the people who are selling it. Viral video is rapidly becoming one of the most powerful ways to market.

- List low. List at least 5% below what you expect to get (the seller above went into escrow at 10% above asking price in 10 days)
- Make sure your property looks good. Stage it and make sure it smells and feels good.
- Create auction type fervor by having a compressed showing 'season' where prospective buyers rub elbows. You might want to have refreshments, and possibly even an appraisal and home inspection sitting out for them to peruse. And tell everyone to simply submit their best offer for review at a later date.

# How to Avoid 7 Deadly and Common Mistakes When You Carry Paper

 *Deadly Mistake #1: Take a small down payment, or none at all.*

Gosh, isn't it amazing the price you can get for your property if you don't ask for a down payment? You can make owning a home cheaper than renting if you want to!

It's OK with me if you take a small down payment to sell quickly for the price you want...just don't be offended when I offer you a small price for your note, or I tell you I can only buy a partial, or that I can't buy it at all.

Why? Because the risk of default is so high. If things got tough, it would be too easy for the buyer to just walk away, because they don't have enough 'skin in the the game'.

And actually, if they can no longer afford the payments, then it would be wonderful if they would just walk away. But normally, they don't. They wait for you to foreclose on them. In California, that can take anywhere from 5-18 months, in other states it can take 2-3 years...ouch.

Sure, you'll get the property back, but after how many missed payments, and after how many legal fees? And will the property be trashed, and/or will the market be even softer when you finally have possession again?

Accepting a small down payment all too often translates into financial loss...there's just not enough of a financial buffer if something goes sideways. It's like sitting on a porcupine and wondering why you're not feeling so cushy and cozy.

**SMART TIP** *Take the largest down payment you can get.*

Getting a 20% down payment will greatly reduce the statistical likelihood of default (and make your note much more valuable). Remember when that's what it took to buy a property? A 10% down payment is usually acceptable for an owner occupied single family residence (O/O SFR).

A down payment creates **Protective Equity**. Protective equity protects the seller (note holder) from financial loss if the buyer (note payor) defaults.

The larger the down payment, the greater the instant equity a buyer has. Think of a down payment as the layer of cream on a fresh cup of milk. The thicker the layer of cream, the richer and tastier it is (and the more you'll have to fight your brother for it).

If you get a 20% down payment or more, then you'll have a note that's worth holding or selling. It'll be rich and tasty, and note buyers will fight each other for the chance to buy it (which translates into a higher price/smaller discount, right?).

If you're going to take a small down payment, you'll want to find a way to reduce or eliminate your exposure to foreclosure (or the risk that a note buyer will have if they buy your note).

Perhaps you'll want to create two notes instead of one (and only sell the first), or use the Title Holding Land Trust to avoid foreclosure altogether.

*Deadly Mistake #2: Don't ask for the buyer's SS#* and don't run a credit report, (or, if you've actually done these things, try to lose the credit application and report so it's unavailable to give a prospective note buyer).

There have been a few times I've been able to offer a really good price for a note, just to have the deal fall apart because the note holders couldn't come up with social security numbers for the Payors.

The investors out there that will pay the most for your note (ask you to take the smallest discount) will want you to have a Social Security number on the buyers (note Payors), and they'll want their **FICOs to be 620 or above**.

There are note buyers out there that will buy your note even if you don't have the buyer's SS#, but they'll probably be offering you a LOT LESS for your note.

And even a great note by all other accounts will be hard to sell if the Payors' credit scores are low. **It's almost impossible to sell a note where the FICOs are coming in below 600.**

Why? Because, statistically speaking, the lower the credit score, the greater the chances that the buyer (note payor) will default.

*Have the buyer provide their SS# by filling out a credit application (1003) and signing it, run credit, and if it doesn't come back above 620, run from the deal, unless...*

There are always ways to compensate for the risk of lending (your equity) to a buyer with poor credit, but still, it's a tough conversation with credit scores in the 500's.

If you're going to do the deal anyway, be sure to take a larger-than-average down payment, and be willing to season the note (collect **at least** 12 months of payments) before trying to sell your note if you want a decent price for it. You might even want to work with the Payors to improve their credit scores before you put your note on the market. (I know someone who is very good at helping people improve their credit scores in a very short period of time, call me).

And even if you're not thinking of selling your note, don't you want a strong investment that doesn't have you addicted to Milk of Magnesia? Don't you want to leave a good asset to your heirs and beneficiaries?

Putting your transaction together in a way that will make your paper (note) valuable on the secondary market will automatically ensure that you've placed yourself in the most powerful position possible, no matter what happens down the road. It provides the most flexibility long term.

If the down payment is small, and the buyer's credit scores are low, then I **HIGHLY RECOMMEND** that you consider using the Title Holding (Land) Trust. (But only if you don't plan on cashing out. You can't sell a beneficial interest in a trust the same way you can sell a note).

☠ *Deadly Mistake #3: Lose the original note.*

The original note is the "green stuff," it's the currency, it's "the thing you're selling;" it's a negotiable instrument. A copy just won't do! The original John Henry (signature) of the Buyer/Payor, even if it's not very attractive, fluid or sophisticated, is the silver lining in your paper.

Losing the original note is akin to committing Original Sin all over again, and do you really want that on your conscience? Won't you have enough to worry about on Judgement Day?

And it kind of makes sense, doesn't it? Would you be able to pay your mortgage by sending in a nice photocopy of your check to Bank of America?  Or the Federal Government? (Wait, they don't own all of the real assets in the country yet, do they?  Sorry, got ahead of myself).

I was recently working with a probate attorney in Los Angeles who was liquidating an estate holding a $500,000 seller carry back note secured by a commercial property.

I was able to offer the estate more than the Payor on the note was offering, so we were ready to open escrow, but none of the heirs/beneficiaries could find the original note.  And that put the estate/note holder in a very awkward position. The Payor could potentially cause problems if he found out and wanted to contest the loan.

So, instead of alerting the Payor that they couldn't find the original note and asking him to sign a new one, (which he probably would have refused to do) they just decided to go the path of least resistance and let him refinance them off at a lower price than they could have gotten if they'd had all their ducks in a row.

 *Keep your ORIGINAL note in a safe place.*

And while you're at it, place all the other important note documents right alongside it:
- copy of the deed of trust or mortgage
- buyers credit application (1003)
- buyers credit score
- escrow instructions
- escrow closing statement/HUD-1 settlement statement
- title insurance (you should have a lender's policy)
- hazard insurance documents (you're the Loss Payee, right?)

If I'm buying your note, I want to be the legal holder of the note, so I need the original note in my possession, and the note properly endorsed to me: ("For value received, Pay to the Order of Dawn Rickabaugh" and it must be signed and dated by the Note Seller).

If the original note is in my possession, and is properly endorsed to me, then I am a holder-in-due-course, which gives me some substantial protection should any legal issues arise.

In some cases where the original note cannot be found, you can purchase a bond, but it's expensive. In essence, a third party company may be willing to insure the payment on a note that can't be located, but they'll charge you through the nose for it.

 *Deadly Mistake #4: Make the interest rate on the note nice and low.*

It's tempting to offer a low interest rate to entice a buyer to give you a fat, juicy price for your property. It's OK if that gets the job done and you're happy with it, but you just have to know that you're writing in the discount you will ultimately take on your note.

Don't write a seller financed note at 5%, amortized over 30 years, and then get offended when a note buyer offers you 60 cents on the dollar. They're not being mean or predatory, it's just the natural consequence of how you structured your deal.

Perhaps you're happy making 5% on your money…if so, great, sit back and collect those payments! But no experienced note investor will buy a note at a 5% yield. They're going to want a minimum of 9-12%. There are only 3 companies in the country that want to buy a 5% note at face value. That's

Fannie Mae, Freddie Mac, and FHA, and none of them are going to buy a seller financed note.

There is usually no reason to give a borrower, who may not even be able to get a conventional loan, the same kind of low rate they could get with the best bank loan out there. This only benefits the borrower.

There may be a way to create more than one note to meet client objectives...one that is meant for sale, one that is meant for long term holding. Each situation is entirely unique and has it's own set of possibilities and limitations.

For a consultation to customize a solution in your particular situation (and if you're a Realtor, to CYA) hire me to take a look.

**SMART TIP** *Charge at least 2-3% more than the market rate.*

If you're going to take back a note (especially if you want it to be worth something on the secondary market) charge the highest interest rate that you can, without violating usury laws, of course.

Sellers will say, "The buyer said they could get 5.25% from Bank of America, so I gave them 5%."

Why would they ask you to carry the financing if they could get 5.25%? They probably couldn't, and even if they could, you should charge a premium (more than the going rate) for the ease of the financing you're providing and the closing costs you're saving them.

So, if a typical buyer can get a 6% 30-year-fixed down at the local bank, then you should shoot for at least 8-9%. This not only gives you a fair return for the service you're providing and the risk you're taking, but also greatly decreases any discount that you will take when you go to sell your note.

But sometimes, buyers have you over a barrel. They'll say, "Take it or leave it…if you won't give me the terms I'm asking for, I'll go to the next desperate seller hanging out there on the market and get what I want."

It's not that charging a low interest rate is bad, or the wrong thing for you to do, you just have to go into the deal with your eyes wide open and know what you really need, now and into the future.

☠ *Deadly Mistake #5: Create a short-term balloon.*

Because of the Time Value of Money (TVM), which says that money to be received sooner is more valuable than money to be received later, it can seem like putting in a 5 year balloon is a good thing. No need to wait 30 long years for payoff, right?

In previous markets, this made a lot of sense. The market was going up, and financing was cheap and easy to get. It was simple to refinance. But now it's a different story, isn't it?

A balloon only adds value to a note when there's a clear and obvious exit strategy, which means easy, available and cheap financing laying around for the Payor to scoop up (or evidence that they have the cash to pay it off).

So, you have this balloon…what's going to happen 5 years down the road if property values have decreased? What if interest rates are high? What if something has happened to the buyer's (Payor's) credit score?

They probably won't be able to refinance and pay you off, so now you're stuck with either restructuring the note or foreclosing and taking the property back.

Most note buyers these days buy a note with a balloon anticipating that they'll end up restructuring the loan and extending the repayment period, which decreases the return (which means they'll need to buy it at a steeper discount than you would normally think, based on the calculations of your nifty little HP).

To ensure that the Payor's have the best chance of being able to refinance when the balloon is due or sooner, make sure they're working on improving their credit score.

 *Fully amortize your note over the shortest time period possible...*

Can the buyer afford a 15-year amortization? Or a 20? When a note is fully amortized (meaning it's completely paid off by the end of the term), we don't have to worry about the buyer's future ability to refinance a balloon payment.

If you're going to ask for a balloon, push it out to 7, 10, or 12 years. The longer we have for the real estate and credit markets to stabilize, the better.

Investors will think..."OK, things are not great now, but I'm pretty sure in 10-12 years the market will have recovered and we'll be in a better situation. By then, this Payor should have no trouble refinancing, especially since the principal balance on the note will be a lot smaller."

Another idea is to ask for Stepped Payments. This is where the interest rate remains the same, but the monthly payment due from the buyer increases by a certain amount or percentage every year. This leads to a faster pay down of the loan balance.

Stepped Payments also provide seniors, who are often on fixed finances at retirement, a stream of income that helps them deal with inflation and the reduced buying power that their money will have with each passing year.

**P.S.  Avoid 'interest-only' loans...
no one wants to buy them!**

 *Deadly Mistake #6: Fail to include a provision for
late payments and a due on sale clause to your note.*

A couple I talked to recently had a one-year-old note that they were trying to sell.  Not only were the terms of the note difficult to understand, but it failed to include a late payment charge, and didn't have a due on sale clause.

"But yes!" they insisted, "see right here in the escrow instructions?  It definitely states that the late payment fee for missed payments is 6%."

Well, it's comforting that you had great intentions, but apparently escrow failed to incorporate your instructions into the note documents, and you didn't notice!  Oops.

*HEADS' UP: escrow companies, title companies, real estate
professionals, accountants and attorneys do not always
know much about putting together a strong note and
calculating the numbers correctly; and unless they regularly
buy and sell notes in the secondary market, (even if they
can accurately print out amortization schedules), they
usually do not understand the financial significance of
how the transaction is engineered.  That's why working
with an owner financing / note professional
will save you thousands...CALL ME!*

Without a late payment provision, you have no way of covering yourself for financial losses when you have a Payor that regularly pays late.

Without a due on sale clause, the property could be sold and you could be receiving payments from someone you haven't had the chance to underwrite (determine if they're a good risk or not). Also, what if interest rates are higher? Wouldn't you like the chance to improve your return?

**SMART TIP** *Make sure your note includes a late payment fee, and make sure the note and deed contain the due on sale (acceleration or alienation) clause.*

You'll have to check with the guidelines in your state, but usually a 6% late fee with a 10-15 day grace period is acceptable.

Put the due on sale clause in both the note and security instrument (deed of trust or mortgage). It might sound something like this:

*If the trustor shall sell, convey or alienate said property, or any part thereof, or any interest therein, or shall be divested of his title in any manner or way, whether voluntarily or involuntarily, without the written consent of the beneficiary being first had and obtained, beneficiary shall have the right, at its option, to declare any indebtedness or obligations secured hereby, irrespective of the maturity date specified in any note evidencing the same, immediately due and payable.*

Also, if it's permitted by law, include a **prepayment penalty** if you're trying to defer capital gains and don't want to be paid off early. Generally things are more regulated for residential properties that serve as the Payor's primary residence. It's usually easy to enforce a prepayment penalty on investment and commercial properties.

The **Deferred Sales Trust** is also a great way to defer capital gains without an exchange and is popular for clients with highly appreciated assets.

*Deadly Mistake #7: Don't keep a careful accounting of the note payments you receive.*

Let's pretend that you have a nice juicy note you're trying to sell...you got a 20% down payment from a buyer who had a 700 FICO, the loan amount was $100,000 at 12% interest. Fully amortized over 20 years, you're supposed to be enjoying $1,101.09 a month.

Wow, isn't that great? Wouldn't you be able to sell that baby for a nice fat price? C'mon...with an average discount, someone's looking to bag a 14% return, for heaven's sake!

Yeah...unless the payments don't come in on time. You could have a 42.9% interest rate, but it doesn't matter, the return is irrelevant if the money isn't flowing.

When someone buys a note (or if you are holding a note for retirement income) the most important thing they want to know is how likely it is that future payments will continue to be paid as agreed.

Most note buyers (the ones that will give you the best price) are not buying hoping they'll get a chance to foreclose and own the property. They just want a predictable return.

***That's why payment history is so important to document.***

Now, if you've got a note that's in default, the only people who will buy it are the ones that wouldn't mind owning the property securing the note, and they'll ask you to take a really steep discount for rescuing you from the foreclosure scenario.

**SMART TIP** *Have a note servicing company service your note if you're too ADD to keep flawless records yourself.*

Document when the payments come in, keep copies of cancelled checks and bank statements so you won't have any trouble proving that you've got a **'performing asset'**.

It's really not a bad idea to have your note serviced by a third party note servicing company. It's not expensive, and your payment history is flawless, which is very handy when you go to sell your note. They also file any relevant documents for you, such as 1098s and 1099s.

Any time there's a 'wrap,' you must have a servicing or escrow company to keep everybody honest!

****************

*Stuff that needs to be in every note:*
- Origination date (should be the same date as the security instrument: deed of trust or mortgage)
- Date interest begins
- Date the first payment is due (and how often – monthly? quarterly?)
- Term and maturity date and/or the date a balloon payment is due and it's estimated amount
- Principal amount of the note (face amount)
- Name of the Payors/Borrowers/Buyers
- Name of the Payees/Lenders/Sellers
- Location where payments are to be sent
- Interest rate
- Exact dollar amount of the payment to be made in each period "or more" if there is no prepayment penalty

- Attorney's fee clause (so you can be reimbursed for legal fees if you have to sue to enforce the terms of the not

More stuff you want in a note, especially if you're the seller:

- Late charge provision, usually 6% with a 10 day grace period
- Due on sale clause, so if the property is sold, you have the right, but not the obligation to 'call' the loan (demand total payment) or renegotiate the terms of the loan
- Prepayment penalty (if you don't want capital gains – just check on the laws in your state. Sometimes a prepayment penalty isn't allowed)

*Most people sleep better if they've had a note professional look over everything before the ink is dry. There are 3 major components to making sure a note is worth holding or selling:*

1. *How the transaction is engineered*

2. *Core mechanical note details*

3. *Documentation needed to properly underwrite the buyer*

# Once I have a great note, how can I sell it?

The best way for me to get you the most accurate quote on your note is to have these documents in front of me:

- the note (crucial)
- the deed or mortgage (very important)
- escrow instructions and/or
- escrow closing statement
- payor's SS#'s (I don't have to have these, but you'll take a MUCH smaller discount if you have your Payors' SS#'s. We'll eventually need to pull a credit report – if you didn't keep them with an original application, your CPA probably has them from filing 1098's and 1099's. If the FICO's come in low, you may want to consider working with your Payors to improve their credit so you can get a better price for your note)

My fax # is: (626)451-0454 (or email me: support@notequeen.com)

[But please, save yourself some time. If you've posted your note on an ebay-type internet auction site, I won't be able to work with you...but I will wish you the very best. And if you're a note broker and want to work with me, then please review my policies at http://notequeen.com/the-way-i-work-with-other-note-brokers/]

Be thinking about how much cash you really need. Are you open to selling a part of your note? You will often have greater success with a "partial." The discount will generally be smaller, and there are more buyers for your note. You can get some cash up front, but then still have payments coming to you down the road. Just something to think about.

> *"What I really appreciate is that you taught us that*
> *we could sell part of our real estate note. No one else*
> *gave us as many options as you did. You helped us*
> *get the money we needed without giving up too big*
> *of a discount. When I want to sell more of this note,*
> *you're the first person I'll call. Thanks a million."*
>
> – Dennis H.

The discount required depends on many different factors. YOU ultimately determined the value and marketability of your note when you created it. That's why it's so important to consult with a note professional BEFORE you close the deal!

There is no 'standard discount.' The discount you will have to take when you sell your note depends on multiple factors: type and location of property, amount of protective equity, priority of the note (is it a 1st or a 2nd?), cost of dealing with a potential foreclosure, payment history, credit and financial strength of the payor, trends in the local real estate market where the security is located, trends in the national economy, yahdah, yahdah, yahdah...

Sellers who carry back paper (and the agents, escrow, title, attorneys and CPA's who advise them) often do not understand the secondary trust deed market. If there are lethal weaknesses in your note, or in the way your transaction was set up, then you probably won't have the option of selling your note at all. Just hang on and hope the buyer keeps making those payments!

**Is the Note Queen a note buyer, or a note broker?**

The answer is: "both." I occasionally buy notes for my own portfolio (just like I occasionally buy properties for my own portfolio), but frequently I function as a note broker, and I can do so in a couple of ways:

1. I can offer you a price for your note, OR
2. I can list your note, like a Realtor lists property

**In real estate...**there are people who want to sell their property FSBO and find their own buyer and do their own paperwork. They take their chances getting into escrow with someone who might not be able to close, and they believe they are sophisticated enough to negotiate all aspects of the transaction, and keep themselves on top of all the paperwork and legalities.

Alternatively, there are people who want a real estate broker to help them package their home for sale, find the buyer that will pay the most for it, and guide and protect them every step of the way.

Statistics show that even paying a commission, most sellers net more by working with a broker, and the process is less stressful and cumbersome.

**In the note world...**people who have notes to sell can do it FSBO. They can do all the research and dig through the maze of institutional and other buyers that might make a bid on their note. They can post their note on an ebay-type service and take calls and emails from hoards of "buyers," most of whom have very little experience, and are brokers disguised as buyers.

These FSBO note sellers take their chances getting under contract with someone who has the reputation for doing the ol' bait-and-switch. (Get you under contract at a high price fully intending to reduce the offer after the due diligence process regardless of what they find.)

Or they'll pull the plug entirely (not unlike banks just before close of escrow). Here's a gem from a 2009 interview with Clint Hinman, veteran of the note industry:

**Clint:** There are still a lot of companies out there that will price deals, but, if you look at what they've acquired, if you could ever take a look into the books and see what they're actually buying, you'll find that they are pretending to still be a valid player in the industry. I won't mention names but I could list at least 5 companies like that right now that still advertise in the newsletters, still show up at all the conventions, send out marketing pieces to all these brokers nationwide, and haven't bought a single note this year.

**NQ: Why are they doing that, Clint?**

**Clint:** Because they're waiting for the market to get better and they don't want to lose their exposure in the meantime.

It is true that the initial quote I give you for a note will have to be reduced if, during the due diligence process, I discover that you have intentionally or unintentionally misrepresented material facts, such as payor's credit, value of property, etc., but the bait-and-switch people have a different agenda.

FSBO note sellers will have to understand that they need to cover themselves in the area of recourse. (Do you want to be on the hook for guaranteeing the note payments after you've sold it at a discount?) **Make sure you know how to read contracts if you're going it alone.**

Many find the note selling process foreign and overwhelming, and would rather pay someone they trust and enjoy working with a reasonable fee to help them understand the process, package their note, and find the buyer that will pay the most for it.

These sellers often net the same or more than when selling FSBO, and definitely find the process much more palatable.

*[REALTORS, CPAS AND ATTORNEYS: you have a fiduciary responsibility to your client, why would you refer your client to a note buyer that is buying for their own portfolio? That might cost your client several thousand dollars. It is far better for your professional reputation to refer a client with a note to someone who will list their note to get them the highest possible price. There are many types of private and institutional buyers out there, and if you haven't been around the block for a while, you don't know how to scare up the best price for a note, guaranteed.]*

When someone is selling a property, I educate them about their options and their ability to sell creatively and carry paper, thereby achieving their objectives more readily.

When someone is selling a note, I educate them about the different ways they can sell a note. They can sell part of the note, or all of it. They can sell a payment stream, or just the balloon. They can sell half of each payment to raise the cash they need now and still have some money coming in.

If it turns out that you aren't able to sell your note, or the discount is just too steep, you can hire me to help you pursue alternatives...perhaps there's something you just haven't thought of.

When Realtors refer buyers or sellers to one another, they pay each other referral fees, usually 25%. When someone refers a note to me that I end up listing or buying, then I pay referral fees exactly the same way.

**Side note** [hey – anyone wanna buy this note?]

Many of the traditional buyers of privately held mortgages have tightened their buying requirements, making it difficult to get a quote on any note that contains so much as a freckle.

They won't look at it if the face value of the note is higher than the value of the property (big problem these days), or if the Payor's credit is below 600 (challenging), or if the Payor has missed even a single payment in 15 years.

I can usually find a home for notes that others turn away. Call me: (626)292-1875.

# EXCLUSIVELY for Realtors...
## QUIT WALKING AWAY FROM COMMISSIONS!

- You have listings you can't take
- Listings expiring unsold
- Sellers stuck on price
- Buyers (or properties) that don't qualify
- An escrow falling apart
- Especially on jumbo residential or commercial
- Become an Owner Financing Expert, or hire one

You most likely have several ideas in your head about owner financing: it's risky, my seller won't be able to get cash, it's hard for me to get paid!

Even if you know a lot about owner financing...

If you don't regularly buy and sell notes, then you don't know how to create a note that's worth maximum value on the secondary market, because things are changing all the time. What worked last year, doesn't work this year.

When a seller offers terms, they can still walk away with cash. If I'm involved in the underwriting process, notes can sometimes be created and immediately sold. There are many ways to use notes and private money to meet client objectives.

Banks have whole underwriting departments...when your client is the bank on their own property, they need to hire a personal underwriter...that's me.

If we're talking about commercial property, I have hedge and private equity funds that are doing the deals the banks just can't pull off. They also do commercial loan workouts. Call me.

# The simultaneous note sale – myth or reality?

A simultaneous note sale, or 'simo,' is when a seller carry back note is sold as soon as it's created. The seller offers owner financing and creates a note for the buyer, and immediately turns around and sells that note to a note buyer the same day. That way the seller walks away with cash even though they've offered terms.

This strategy was popular and worked really well when everything was 'functioning' in the credit markets, including sub prime and option ARMs.

Clint Hinman, President of Proficient Note Buyers and former editor of Noteworthy, was kind enough to spend a few minutes on the phone with me and share his perspective on simos. I'll print part of that interview here. It's excellent, and Clint is one of the most honest, upstanding and generous leaders in the note industry today.

**NQ: So, what's the deal with simos? They've pretty much disappeared in the last couple of years, haven't they?**

**Clint:** Well, the biggest difference between two to three years ago and today is who has the upper hand in the buyer/ seller relationship. Right now, it's a buyer's market. Brokers of notes and sellers of properties no longer have the leverage they once had.

When Mortgage Backed Securities were the rule of the day, these companies were starved for product. They were buying up anything and everything that they could buy. Simply put, there wasn't enough product just relying on old-fashioned seller financed notes that had been seasoned for 3, 4, 10 years.

So the only way to get more product was to create more product. The simultaneous closing, although it wasn't necessarily created at that point, became much more prevalent because now these companies were pushing real estate investors to create the notes as quickly as they could. They'd buy them fresh off the block, and push them into a security right away.

There was very little risk of default while they held it because obviously they pushed them off into securities and somebody else absorbed the risk. And of course that was what was happening with more than just these simultaneous seller finance closings. This is what was happening with the sub-prime mortgages as well.

In essence, you were just putting a bunch of hooey in a security, calling it Triple A, thanks to the rating agencies, and selling it to pension funds half a world away who had really no idea what really stood behind their securities.

**NQ: Okay, so now there's basically nobody out there doing simultaneous closings anymore...like nobody?**

**Clint:** Right. There's no market for it, and most of the niche buyers that survived this latest debacle want seasoning. They want the borrowers to show that they have the willingness and the ability to make payments before they'll touch the note.

**NQ: For how long?**

**Clint:** It typically depends on the parameters of the note. With good credit, a really strong third-party-verified down payment and payment history, secured by a plain vanilla-type property, some will buy with as little as 1-3 months' seasoning, but I will tell you that I just updated Noteworthy's database of note investors and without exception, everybody asked that we remove simultaneous closings from the types of notes they'd buy.

**NQ: And for the buyers who are still out there buying them, it seems that the discounts are pretty hefty, aren't they?**

**Clint:** They are. Again, it's all a matter of credit, equity, or loan-to-value. Real estate investors that go into a property and pay $20,000 for it, do minimal fix up or rehab, and then sell it for $60,000 can't figure out why investors won't buy their note after 3 months.

And it's typically because the valuations on the property don't hold up because a Realtor and appraiser can see that it was sold just a few months earlier for far less than it was resold for. So, obviously note investors don't want to be caught holding the bag on notes secured by properties that are far over-valued from what they're really worth.

Most note buyers have a 12-month seasoning requirement on rehab-type flipper paper. It's separate from your traditional 'mom and pop America' selling a property to maybe their renter. So, I want to point that out…rehab paper is looked at completely differently than your traditional seller financed note.

**[To get the entire interview with Clint, order "Flip With Owner Financing" from www.NoteQueen.com. It's your updated road map and will save you thousands of dollars and many, many hours! It's a 'must-have' for today's real estate investor.]**

****************

It seems like the 'mom and pop' paper (after 1-3 months) can get somewhere between 70 to 80 cents on the dollar, starting with an 80% LTV (loan-to-value) note. If there's only a 10% cash down payment available from the buyer, it would be wise for the seller to create a 10% 2nd so they could preserve a little more of their asset.

A note investor doesn't seem to want to be in for much more than 60% ITV (investment-to-value), so the smaller the note, the less of a discount the note seller will take. Selling a 'partial' is also a great way to minimize the discount required.

You may be able to do a true 'simo' (a double escrow) with a local investor, but even so, they usually aren't crazy about rehab paper. [In Southern California, Texas, Georgia and Missouri I can sometimes put simos together...email me!]

*Quick Story...*

How the simultaneous note sale (the creating and selling of notes) can get sellers the highest possible price in today's market, and their agents the best possible commissions:
- Listing price (commercial property): $900,000
- Offer: $900,000 with $200,000 down payment
- Buyer could not get bank financing
- Investor offered to buy the $700,000 note immediately for $575,000 (in a double escrow).

This would have netted the seller $775,000 minus closing costs, and the agents' commissions would have been based upon a $900,000 sales price.

The agents didn't understand seller financing and note sales, so they refused to bring the conversation up with their client. Here's what they did instead:
- Dropped the listing price to $600,000 to get an all-cash buyer that didn't need financing.

- Seller, instead of $775,000, walked away with only $600,000, and
- Commissions were based on a $600,000 sale.

Seller lost $175,000 and agents lost 30% of their commissions because they were not open to learning about how seller financing and subsequent note sales could benefit their client (and them!).

****************

I know of local investors who have come together in their communities who ARE buying rehab paper after 3-4 months of seasoning (not the 12+ usually required) through their self-directed IRAs when a note professional is underwriting the transaction.

They are happy to have their money out of the stock market, and making a solid, much more predictable return of 8-10% through investing in real estate and notes.

Buyers are putting down at least 10% and demonstrate the ability to pay, and all investors are investing in the communities where they live, and this allows them to accomplish locally what would be impossible for a nationally based investment company.

These investors are the life blood of the economy, and I hope the "SAFE" Mortgage Act doesn't prevent them from providing home ownership to thousands of families who just can't qualify for institutional financing.

In Texas, Missouri and Georgia (because foreclosure takes about 5 minutes) I have a guy that will do true simultaneous closings on genuinely rehabilitated properties. Order '**Flip With Owner Financing**' to get the details.

****************

Some Realtors are making seller financing their primary niche. They routinely profit from buyers that other agents don't know how to work with.

If you're a real estate professional and you have past clients that carried paper on the sale of a property or business, (or clients that are in the process of offering owner financing right now) then you can make a referral fee when I buy their note... let's talk. Chances are, your client may not even even know they have the option to sell their note, and in this economy, people are looking for cash everywhere they can find it.

If you're in an investor looking to flip with owner financing, consider hiring me to underwrite your transactions so you can keep up to date with what's happening on the secondary market.

### Story Time (Realtors, pay attention):

A guy found me on the internet not too long ago, and he wanted to sell his note. He had sold his landscaping business 3 months previously, and now wanted to free up some cash to invest in short sales.

After we talked briefly about the mechanics of the transaction, I said, "Oh, I wish we'd had this chat before you closed, it would have made your note a lot easier to sell, and the discount a lot smaller."

*"I asked my agent if he knew anyone that could help put the note together, and he said no!"*

He was pretty exasperated at this point. Then when I got a copy of his closing documents, we discovered that not only was the transaction engineered poorly, but the note had errors to boot!

The dates and numbers just didn't match up (remember what I said about escrow companies not always knowing how to craft a good note?), now I'm not sure I can get a buyer for this note at any price! Additionally, the agent failed to make sure that they ran the buyer's credit...WOW.

**If you're supposed to be the professional, don't let yourself look like a fool. You just might find yourself in a lawsuit down the road. Hire me to be your underwriting department.**

# How To Avoid
# Life-Throttling Capital Gains

**DOES ANY OF THIS SOUND FAMILIAR?**

**"I would sell my property, but I can't because..."**

- *I refuse to pay all those capital gains*...and I don't want to exchange into another property because I'm tired of managing property and dealing with tenants.

- *I need the income*...this is my retirement!

- *It's a bad time to sell*...I won't get a good price.

- I've got tenants/family members that don't pay me enough, but I just don't have the heart to raise their rent or kick them out.

- *I want to give my children a good inheritance.* I'm leaving the rental properties to them... we already have a trust set up.

If you hear yourself in any of the above, (or you hear this from clients that won't give you the listing) keep reading. This section will expand your understanding, and give you more options than you may have previously thought possible.

Many people have wisely invested in real estate over the years to achieve their financial objectives. Acquiring income-producing property is one of the best ways to create wealth.

However, at some point, many people tire of managing their properties. They are tired of dealing with tenants and the necessary repairs. Perhaps health problems are forcing them to slow down. They want smart, safe investments that are less management intensive so they can relax, travel, and enjoy life.

With Seller Financing, you can DO LESS and GET MORE, turning your best investment into an even better one. Seller Financing can turn real estate into a paper asset secured by real property. Structured properly, this is one of the safest, most coveted investments in the market today.

If you own nothing more than your own primary residence, this information can be extremely valuable when the time comes for you to sell. I'll address this more in detail later on, but for now, let's get started!

And for you real estate professionals, you've got to become more than a salesperson...you've got to become a **TRUSTED ADVISOR** to your clients. If you don't tell them about deferring capital gains when they're selling investment property, you could lose your license (at least that's what I heard from an agent in Colorado...gotta **at least** mention a 1031 exchange, for heaven's sake, but why stop there?) Why not prove how invaluable you are as an information resource to your client?

*The best ways to defer capital gains:*

There are actually many strategies for deferring capital gains...several exit strategies when disposing of real estate that help you escape a massive tax bill and maximize your income for retirement:

- **Installment Sale – (Seller Financing)**
- **Title Holding (Land) Trust**
- **1031 Exchange**
- **Deferred Sales Trust**
- **Lease Option or Lease Purchase**

I won't be talking about the last one, because I do not recommend it as a general rule. You can get the benefits of a Lease Option without the risks through the Title Holding (Land) Trust. And let's face it…when we're dealing with your retirement income, we can't afford to be sloppy.

The Installment Sale and the Title Holding (Land) Trust both help a property seller **GET TOP DOLLAR**, because you are offering terms. When buyers don't need a loan from a bank to buy your property, then there are more of them fighting for it, which pushes price up.

The 1031 Exchange and the Deferred Sales Trust require a buyer to pay all cash, or to be able to get a bank loan. Many times this means that you will not get the highest price for your property, but you're free and clear of it.

### Installment Sale – (Seller Financing)

In case you skipped to this section about capital gains without reading the first part, I'll briefly recap seller financing here.

Seller Financing is when a seller becomes the bank (the beneficiary) by acting as a lender to finance all or part of the sale of their own property. The seller is literally "carrying back," or "carrying paper," on the property being sold.

Instead of a buyer giving the seller a down payment and getting a loan from a bank for the rest, the buyer gives the seller the down payment AND the monthly payments.

The seller receives payments according to the terms agreed to in a Promissory Note, which is secured by a Deed of Trust (in California) against the seller's property until the note is paid off.

Seller Financing applies to all types of real estate: homes, land, mobile homes on land, apartment buildings, condos, office buildings, farms, commercial, industrial, and warehouse properties to name a few.

## *Why would anyone carry back paper?*

Many people (including professionals) mistakenly believe that only desperate sellers agree to carry paper and finance the sale of their own property. While it is true that some sellers (who would rather have all cash) carry the financing just to get their property sold in a rough market, many sellers use Seller Financing ON PURPOSE!

*Here are some of the benefits of owner financing:*
- Defer capital gains
- Get full market price and close
  quickly by offering terms
- Have twice as many buyers
  interested in your property
- Get a good cash down payment now
- Collect hassle-free monthly income for years
- Your note is secured by a property you
  understand and whose value you know
- Sometimes you get more each month
  than you could collect in rent
- Never worry about dealing with tenants
  or maintaining the property
- Pay no more property taxes or insurance
- Ideally you will have a note you can sell in whole or
  in part if you (or your heirs) ever need cash down
  the road

Let's face it…federal capital gains will probably be going up. For this reason, more and more people are looking for ways to avoid paying them.

When someone in California sells a non-owner-occupied investment property (or a high end luxury home) they will have to pay a 25% capital gains tax. For example, someone who makes a $400,000 profit on the sale of their rental may immediately owe the government $100,000 right off the top.

**OUCH!!!**

Historically, many people have used the 1031 Exchange. They can defer 100% of their capital gains indefinitely using this technique, moving from one type of investment property to another.

But a 1031 Exchange can be complicated, and a lot of sellers just want out of real estate all together. They just don't want another property to deal with.

According to IRC 453, the Installment Sale (Carrying Back a Note through Seller Financing) allows you to defer capital gains as well. You only pay capital gains on the amount of principal you collect each year.

Because you are receiving the payment for your property in installments (a little at a time), the IRS allows you to pay your taxes in installments (a little at a time). You will pay capital gains on the down payment you receive, and then on the amount of principal you receive in each subsequent year.

Many people think that they need all cash when they sell a piece of property, but do they? Some do, some don't. What most people need, more than a huge pile of cash, is income. If you had enough income on a regular basis, would you need a large chunk of change all at once?

Carrying the financing does not mean you can't walk away with cash at the close of escrow. Many people don't need all of their cash out, but they usually want enough to cover closing costs, and maybe a few thousand to buy a new car, pay off credit cards, or put a new roof on their primary residence. If I'm **involved in the underwriting**, I can find the perfect solution to meet both sellers' and buyers' needs.

Make sure to read the section on the 7 Deadly Mistakes and Smart Tips in previous chapters.

### *Never worry about dealing with tenants or maintaining the property*

When you use the Seller Financing technique, you become the banker, not the owner. As the note holder, you will never receive a phone call from tenants, or have to worry about replacing the roof.

**Many people are concerned about leaving a great inheritance.**

Maybe they've promised to leave certain properties to each of their heirs, and have even set up a trust.

Owners who are worried about leaving a good inheritance behind often do not consider what a great asset a note is, especially one that is secured by a first deed of trust. It is just as easy to leave a note to heirs as it is to leave them a piece of real estate. Notes can be held in a trust just like property is.

In fact, a note can be a superior asset depending on the person doing the inheriting. Instead of inheriting something that needs to be managed, they simply inherit a hassle-free stream of monthly income that they could sell in whole or in part when they need extra cash.

**But what about my tenants?**

Many property owners won't sell because they are concerned about their tenants and don't want to displace them. Sometimes family members live in the rental, often paying far below market rents.

Even when owners are struggling financially, they are often reluctant to raise rents or kick these low-paying tenants out because of the emotional repercussions. These owners often feel trapped by the situation.

What can they do?

If you feel protective of your tenants, (you can't bring yourself to raise rents or evict them), there is still a way to sell and get the some of the benefits you're looking for.  Call me.

****************

**Let's say you're ready to sell your primary residence.** You don't have the same capital gains concern (unless the value of your property greatly exceeds your home owner's exemption). Is Seller Financing still something you should consider?

**Without a doubt!**

If you own your property free and clear (or have great underlying financing) you can use Seller Financing to sell your property quickly, for full price, regardless of market conditions. In these times, everyone should evaluate their options for carrying paper.

*The market is still good for flexible sellers!*

For high-end residential properties, home owners can still get slammed with capital gains.  Some are getting around this by using the Installment Sale, the Deferred Sales Trust, or turning their primary residence into an investment for 12-18 months before selling.

Then they get the best of both worlds: home owner's exemption AND the ability to do a 1031 Exchange with the rest of it through proper use of the Title Holding (Land) Trust.

## Title Holding (Land) Trust

The Title Holding Trust may very well be THE BEST vehicle for acquiring, holding and transferring an interest in real estate. Please refer to the previous conversation about trusts earlier in this book.

More than a simple land trust, this is an asset preservation and estate planning system. Here's a reminder of the advantages:

- **It's like the Installment Sale, only better**
- **Never worry about foreclosure; simply evict a defaulting "resident beneficiary"**
- **Get privacy, safety and legal protection**
- **Get the highest possible value from an investment partner because you're offering terms**
- **It's quick and easy (you can often close in 21 days)**
- **Defer 100% of your capital gains and depreciation recapture until the trust is terminated**
- **Sometimes you keep the existing tax basis**
- **Protection from litigation, creditor judgments, tax liens and probate issues**
- **Reduces the risk of taking a small initial contribution**
- **Freezes the seller's equity until some point in the future when housing has begun to**

appreciate again (the seller will get their equity at some point in the future)
- Retain an equitable interest in the property when the buyer's bank won't allow you to record a 2nd seller carry against your property)

The Title-Holding Land Trust (based upon the well-known "Illinois Land Trust") is largely accepted throughout the United States. This revocable, inter-vivos, beneficiary-directed trust may arguably be the best possible means of real property asset preservation and estate planning.

The land trust is unique in that a property's legal and equitable titles are vested in the trustee, rather than in the owner of record. The land trust's beneficiaries remain fully in control of the property and the actions of the trustee.

When there are multiple (unrelated) beneficiaries in the trust, the property and its title become virtually immune to tax liens, creditor judgments, lawsuits and charging orders. Even the IRS can't touch a property in a co-beneficiary land trust.

*The Trust Transfer System Includes:*
1. A simple Land Trust
2. An Assignment of Beneficiary Interest
3. A Beneficiary Agreement
4. An Occupancy Agreement (i.e. a tenancy agreement whereby a co-beneficiary 'leases' from the trust, versus holding a title interest in the property)
5. A Power of Attorney from a non-participating beneficiary to the party handling the management of the property.

When combined, these documents effectively afford a would-be buyer all the benefits of home ownership, including income tax deductions in most instances.

The Title Holding Trust System gives a seller who is willing to leave his equity (or his existing financing) in place a quick, easy and safe method of disposing of the property, while also giving a buyer virtually 100% of the benefits of ownership.

The trust system provides the seller an excellent means of AVOIDING:

- Immediate capital gains and depreciation recapture
- Hefty capital gains on high-end residential properties
- Hanging out in a dead market with a stale listing when properties aren't selling
- Walking away from equity (freeze it and get it later when the market has recovered!)
- Risky seller carry back scenarios (like Lease Option and Contract for Deed)
- The hassle of becoming a landlord with negative cash flow (OUCH!)
- Tenants who will destroy your property
- A state's withholding tax if the trustee is a corporation (at least in California)

## The 1031 Exchange

### What is a 1031 exchange?

Section 1031 of the Internal Revenue Code allows you to dispose of certain real property and defer the payment of your federal, (and in most cases), state depreciation recapture and capital gain income tax liabilities by exchanging the real property (relinquished property) for qualified use "like-kind" property (replacement property).

### Is 1031 exchanging a new concept?

NO. Section 1031 of the Internal Revenue Code was first introduced in 1921. The purpose or intent behind a 1031 exchange is to encourage you to reinvest 100% of your net proceeds into like-kind replacement property when you sell qualifying property.

*What are the benefits of doing an exchange?*

1031 exchange transactions are one of the last remaining strategies available to defer the recognition of capital gain and depreciation recapture income taxes on the sale or disposition of qualifying property.

Usually, when you sell your investment property you will trigger Federal and state capital gain and depreciation recapture income taxes, which will leave you with much less to reinvest.

This makes it extremely difficult for you to trade up in real estate value, increase your cash flow and ultimately your net-worth when you have to recognize and pay these income tax liabilities.

By completing a 1031 exchange you can defer your capital gains and depreciation recapture and keep 100% of your proceeds from the sale of your investment properties available to reinvest in other like-kind replacement properties, especially to trade up in value and improve your cash flow.

But you'll need an all cash or cash-to-new-loan offer, so you'll have to be ready to sell at a lower price than you could get if you were using one of the powerful "Owner Will Carry" strategies like the Installment Sale or the Title Holding (Land) Trust.

### The Deferred Sales Trust

The Deferred Sales Trust (DST) is a product to consider using when you want the **benefits of an installment sale**

- defer capital gains
- get monthly income for retirement

**without the risks of carrying paper.** You'll never have to worry about having to foreclose if the buyer defaults, because the buyer brought you cash (or cash to new loan) to acquire your property.

Your monthly payment is not secured by the property or business, but by the trust itself, which consists of a portfolio that you help define using standard investment vehicles.

You don't have to trust the buyer to pay you, you have to trust:

1. The money managers (you may choose your own)
2. Wall Street and the economy not to collapse entirely

The Deferred Sales Trust takes over where the Private Annuity Trust left off.

**This strategy is gaining popularity among those who have highly appreciated assets, or assets that would be hard to exchange, such as business interests.**

An average transaction deals with $2.4 million in gain that needs to be sheltered from a direct capital gains hit, but should be considered any time there is a gain of $100,000 or more. We are currently working on a trust worth $44,000,000. Investors selling business + real estate (such as a dental practice) commonly use this vehicle.

*Here's the anatomy of the transaction:*

- seller 'sells' his property to a trust managed by a third party company on 100% seller carry installment note
- trust lists and sells the property conventionally (getting cash or CTNL from the buyer)
- trust pays seller with a payment contract called an "installment contract" paid over an agreed period of time (up to 20 years). The returns are usually 3-6%, possibly higher if you define a more aggressive, risk tolerant portfolio with your advisor when the trust is set up.

Deferred Sales Trusts are drafted pursuant to IRC 453, the same as the installment sale in the seller financing scenario. The capital gains tax is realized or triggered, but not recognized or paid (not until the seller starts receiving the payments, and even then capital gains are only paid a little at a time).

**You need to price your property to sell.** If you're not going to offer terms through an Installment Sale, or through a Title Holding (Land) Trust (which helps maximize price point), then you'll have to be very realistic on price. For an illustration of how the DST might work for you, visit www. notequeendst.com.

# Wrapping It Up

By now I hope you feel empowered to get what you need and want regardless of market conditions. This is a time of unparalleled opportunity, and you have options...it's about being informed and choosing the strategies that work best for you and the other parties involved in your transaction. I'm here to help.

I'm always developing materials for real estate professionals, note brokers, buyers and sellers that will teach them how to become Owner Financing Experts...expertise that the market is desperate for. Visit NoteQueen.com to see what I've got available, and watch for the upcoming membership/training site:

*www.OwnerFinancingClub.com*

I'm increasingly being asked to train people in the note business...to help them learn what they really need to know in a fraction of the time, with a fraction of the cost.

I occasionally do free FAQ (frequently asked questions) calls and I'd love to have you join me on Facebook (search for 'Note Queen: Owner Financing Strategies...and when you get there, 'LIKE' it for heaven's sake :-).

Keep an eye on the Events Calendar so you don't miss anything! We're just starting to build our community!

People are learning the Dance Between Property and Paper. Note finders/brokers are discovering more ways to use and profit from the power of the note business. Sellers are increasingly looking for Realtors who understand owner financing, so make sure you're networking here! (That means, leave a comment on the 'wall' so you show up!)

To your success, now and always,

*Dawn*

# APPENDIX
## The SAFE Mortgage Act, HR 4173
## & Other Stuff

Wow...what a time to be alive. Things are certainly not boring! If you're not paying attention, this is a time when your most basic of rights will slip right out from under your nose.

There is quite a mess in the aftermath of the banking crisis because the government has felt compelled to 'fix' things. Ug. How does that make sense when they helped create the mess in the first place?

But it's kind of convenient, because when something disastrous happens and people are scared and hurt, they usually roll over and give up basic rights and agree to larger government...perfect time for a major power grab.

Besides The SAFE Mortgage Licensing Act (which has already become law) there are several bills in the process of being passed, in fact, several versions of several bills, some of which are downright contradictory, so it's an incredibly confusing time out there, even for attorneys good at following this stuff.

### The SAFE Mortgage Licensing Act

The Housing and Economic Recovery Act of 2008, signed into law on July 30, 200 (HERA), constitutes a major new housing law that is supposedly designed to assist with the recovery and the revitalization of America's residential housing market - from modernization of the Federal Housing Administration, to foreclosure prevention, to enhancing consumer protections. The SAFE Act is a key component of HERA.

"The SAFE Act is designed to enhance consumer protection and reduce fraud by encouraging states to establish minimum standards for the licensing and registration of state-licensed mortgage loan originators and for the Conference of State Bank Supervisors (CSBS) and the American Association of Residential Mortgage Regulators (AARMR) to establish and maintain a nationwide mortgage licensing system and registry for the residential mortgage industry." – HUD

Doesn't sound bad, does it? Not until you realize they've potentially lumped small time owner financing in with all the mortgage activities regularly engaged in by large brokerages and lending institutions.

Hey, let's regulate everybody while we're at it! Fun times! Funny thing is, the large institutions seem to be exempt from the licensing requirements…curious.

**Before we go any further, you DO NOT have to worry about the SAFE Act when you're offering terms to someone when you are selling:**
- Your primary residence
- A residential property to a family member
- A residential property to someone who will use it as a rental or vacation home
- Non-residential property
- According to HR 4173 (more on that in a minute), you are allowed to owner finance up to 3 residential properties a year without worrying about licensing

If you're an investor and you've used up your 3 freebies, the SAFE Act suggests that you have to be a licensed mortgage originator (LMO) to sell your residential property with seller financing to someone who intends to use the property as a primary residence .

You'd think at the outside they would say, "OK, if you're going to carry paper on multiple residential properties, then you need to have a LMO (licensed mortgage originator) negotiate the terms and put the appropriate paperwork together for you."

Not so. Technically, as the federal regulation stands, the owner of the properties has to be licensed; however, in some states (Texas, for instance) they've got the state entities to formally grant this concession. Investors can still offer owner financing to families who can't get bank loans if they run their deals through a LMO. Many attorneys agree that this is adequate compliance with the SAFE Act across the board.

So, what about the people who have acquired a small portfolio of properties over the years, and have planned all along to sell with owner financing in order to defer capital gains and create healthy retirement income?

Here's more from HUD:

*"Notwithstanding the broad definition of "loan originator" in the SAFE Act, there are some limited contexts where offering or negotiating residential mortgage loan terms would not make an individual a loan originator. The provision in the definition that loan originators are individuals who take an "application" implies a formality and **commercial context** that is wholly absent where an individual offers or negotiates terms of a residential mortgage loan with or on behalf of a member of his or her immediate family. State legislation that excludes from licensing and registration requirements an individual who offers or negotiates terms of a residential mortgage loan only with or on behalf of*

*an immediate family member will not be found to be*
*out of compliance with the SAFE Act.*

Personally, based on the 'commercial context' mentioned by HUD, if I were selling off a small portfolio of properties (more than 3) I had acquired over the years, or had inherited through an estate, I wouldn't be concerned about the SAFE Act. If I wanted to be super conservative, I might have a LMO process the paperwork for me.

Alternatively, I could use the Title Holding (Land) Trust and get around the whole conversation altogether!

For reference, the SAFE Act defines a residential property as any dwelling with 1-4 units, vacant residential lots (that could potentially be built into homes), mobile homes (this is throwing the mobile home industry into a tailspin), and even trailers (if they're going to be lived in). Way to severely limit the accessibility of low-income housing!

Imagine all those RV retailers who don't know they're in violation of the SAFE Act when they sell a motor home to someone who might end up living out of it! Woohoo! What a ride.

Some unfortunate (and hopefully unintentional) consequences of the legislation is that buyers who can't qualify for bank loans are going to have a harder time acquiring homes for their families.

Banks won't finance them, and government is making sure it's harder (at least more expensive) for investors to finance them. Nice. So is this really about consumer protection or government control? Hmmm.

Here's a gem, once again, from one of my favorite people in the note industry, Clint Hinman:

*"Let's take a snippet from the article I posted on the website today, courtesy of MarketWatch, the Wall Street Journal's online news presence, discussing big banks' intention to pursue profit models internationally, rather than domestically:*

**'Such moves suggest that new financial regulations will make U.S., consumer-focused banking less attractive as returns won't be high enough to justify the cost of the extra capital required to support such businesses.'**

*Huh – sounds like they're saying all this additional regulation will make it impossible to make a profit here in the good 'ol U.S. of A. Gosh oh gee willikers…who'da thunk it? So FrankenDodd's monster of more regulatory oversight is actually hurting consumers? You bet your tax-strapped backside it is. Wait…you didn't really think… oh, this is awkward…you REALLY thought all this hullabaloo was about YOU? Tsk tsk… silly little people. (wink wink nudge nudge)."*

Read the whole post here: http://www.pronotebuyers.com/blog.details.php?id=315

So, banks get the bailout money, but won't lend here in the US…no, they're going to take their taxpayer-funded bailouts and invest them abroad where they can actually make a buck!

Well, what's good for the goose is good for the gander… let's all start investing outside of the US! In fact, why not have a second home in Brazil?

## HR 4173 Infected with HR 1728 Virus

The very pathogenic HR 1728 thankfully got tabled in the senate, but thanks to Dodd-Frank, some of it (albeit a less virulent strain) found it's way into HR 4173 which passed and is waiting to be signed by the president.

The former offending section of HR 1728 is now found in Title XIV of the joint bill :

*TITLE XIV – MORTGAGE REFORM AND ANTI-PREDATORY LENDING ACT – SUBTITLE A – RESIDENTIAL MORTGAGE LOAN ORIGINATION STANDARDS*

*Section 103 of the Truth in Lending Act (15 U.S.C. 1602) is amended by adding at the end the following new subsection:*

*(2) MORTGAGE ORIGINATOR – The term `mortgage originator':*

*(E) does not include, with respect to a residential mortgage loan, a person, estate, or trust that provides mortgage financing for the sale of 3 properties in any 12-month period to purchasers of such properties, each of which is owned by such person, estate, or trust and serves as security for the loan, provided that such loan;*

*(i) is not made by a person, estate, or trust that has constructed, or acted as a contractor for the construction of, a residence on the property in the ordinary course of business of such person, estate, or trust;*

*(ii) is fully amortizing;*

*(iii) is with respect to a sale for which the seller determines in good faith and documents that the buyer has a reasonable ability to repay the loan;*

*(iv) has a fixed rate or an adjustable rate that is adjustable after 5 or more years, subject to reasonable annual and lifetime limitations on interest rate increases; and*

*(v) meets any other criteria the Board may prescribe*

HR 1728 would have only allowed one (1) seller financed sale every 36 months without a license. Now we have nine (9) allowed every 36 months (3 per year). This is a significant improvement...but still not good enough.

Stay tuned and participate in the next CALL TO ACTION that will help preserve our rights and the ability of investors to continue providing housing to families who can't qualify for bank loans.

Follow David Butler. You can find his threads on Creative Real Estate Online: http://www.creonline.com/cashflow/wwwboard3/messages/27103.html

## Replacing Fannie and Freddie's $1.5 Trillion Balance Sheet

Fannie Mae and Freddie Mac provide liquidity (buy) 70% of all residential loans funded in the U.S. That means if it weren't for Fannie and Freddie, 70% of the loans currently being funded today just wouldn't happen.

And good 'ol F&F are finding that they're a day late and a dollar (or two) short. They have no friends in Congress and politicians across the board blame them for creating the housing bubble.

The White House is scheduled to release its plan on what to do with Fannie and Freddie. The Obama administration is already being tarred and feathered by bankers who expect to see their future earnings snipped by 20% or more (thanks to the new regulatory reform bill – thus the attractiveness of those foreign investments!)

While it's easy to stick out your tongue at these wayward twins, here's the rub: If the two eventually disappear, who will fill the financing void?

At last check, Fannie and Freddie had a combined balance sheet of $1.6 trillion, mostly whole loans and MBS (mortgage backed securities). They guarantee $5.5 trillion in residential product, or **55% of all housing debt in the U.S.!!!** If they go away, who takes their place?

Not sure how it'll all shake out, but if we protect our personal property rights adequately, owner financing will continue to help buyers and sellers come together regardless of what's happening in the credit markets. This, of course, strengthens the real estate market and the overall economy in very important ways.

Dawn Rickabaugh is a CA Real Estate Broker specializing in legal, ethical and intelligent alternative financing. She regularly puts and keeps real estate (and small business) transactions together without the need for new bank financing using a combination of owner financing strategies, private money and commercial hedge funds. She is dedicated to liberating & empowering buyers, sellers and real estate professionals in today's market.

She is a writer, educator, coach and consultant. She has been interviewed and quoted by influential publications such as Investor's Business Daily, and Wall Street Journal's MarketWatch.

Because she regularly buys and brokers notes secured by real estate (and businesses) she is powerfully poised to help sellers and their agents understand how to carry paper safely. The note business is constantly changing, so only someone who regularly buys and sells notes knows how to engineer seller financing transactions to create notes worth holding or selling.

She loves teaching intelligent use of the Installment Sale and the Title Holding Trust for maximum benefits, and loves to help sellers find ways to avoid paying life-throttling capital gains.

**When banks say 'NO,' we say 'YES!'**

www.NoteQueen.com

P: 626.292.1875

F: 626.451.0454

support@notequeen.com